THE
Killing Days

KEMAL PERVANIC

BLAKE

Published by Blake Publishing Ltd,
3 Bramber Court, 2 Bramber Road,
London W14 9PB, England

First published in 1999

ISBN 1 85782 363 X

British Library Cataloguing-in-Publication Data:
A catalogue record for this book is available
from the British Library.

Typeset by BCP

Printed in Great Britain by
Creative Print and Design (Wales),
Ebbw Vale, Gwent.

1 3 5 7 9 10 8 6 4 2

Publisher's note
For the benefit of English-speaking readers, certain
Bosnian characters have been anglicized.

Contents

The Killing Days

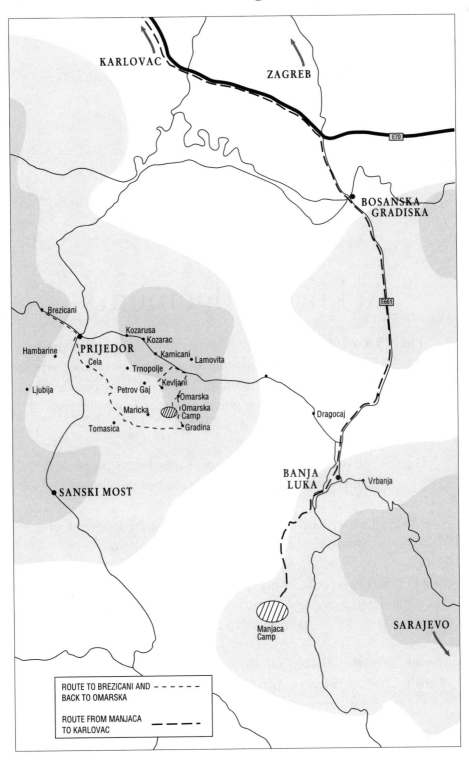

ROUTE TO BREZICANI AND
BACK TO OMARSKA

ROUTE FROM MANJACA
TO KARLOVAC

Dedication

In memory of innocent victims of all wars, past and present.

Acknowledgements

I feel that many people deserve some credit for enabling me
to write this book. To try to name them all would be injustice to those
whose names I might omit to mention. There are a few people who
were directly involved in my work, however, whom I would
like to acknowledge.

Lee Bryant, whose useful comments on the first draft proved
extremely valuable in preparing revised versions.

Jasna Pignon, who tirelessly spent weekend after weekend with
me editing subsequent drafts of the book.

Brian Philips, who unselfishly helped me polish the final draft, and
who has acted ever since as my official publicist, or 'ambassador'
as I prefer to call him.

The whole team at Blake Publishing – John Blake, Rosie Ries, Adam
Parfitt, Charlotte Helyar, Anne Marie Gormley and Ceri Parsons –
who were always very supportive through all stages of publication.

Their friendship has been the most wonderful present I could
get from this work.

Foreword

There's a point when every conflict comes to an end...and somebody always survives. Every conflict has its survivors who live to tell their story, and I will survive this one.

These are the words of Kemal Pervanic, the author of this chilling and powerful book.

We should be thankful that his prediction from his time in Omarska camp during the Bosnian War came true.

The Killing Days is a moving book recalling a terrible and shameful period in Europe's history. All the more so because its simple language recalls the experiences not of a politician, or a general, or a journalist, or an analyst of war, but of one of many hundreds of thousands of anonymous victims of the grand designs of Balkan leaders.

What happened to Kemal Pervanic happened to countless others whose stories may never be told. And to countless more in Kosovo, whose fate is now slowly being disinterred with their remains from the Balkans' latest killing fields.

I was the first person to get into Manjaca camp during the Bosnian War, having been threatened by Serb Generals who tried to stop me that if I went there I would be shot. I saw the prisoners who had previously been in Omarska. Maybe Kemal was among them, though we never met. Certainly the terrible experiences of the prisoners there, of which Kemal writes so movingly, was etched into every one of the emaciated faces I saw – and they haunt me still.

It is a sad irony that within only a few years of the end of the Bosnian conflict the Balkans are again in turmoil. I only hope that at last we will learn, and that the experiences of Kemal – and again of thousands like him in Kosovo – will never be repeated in the name of political or ethnic advantage.

To read this book is to understand, painfully, the human consequences of our failures in the Balkans and the historical necessity of ensuring we never repeat them.

The Rt Hon Paddy Ashdown MP
London 1999

Preface

I remember the Bank Holiday weekend at the end of May 1992 with great clarity and affection. Sunny afternoons in the garden and walks along the Backs in Cambridge. An outing to the cinema. The excitement of making a home with my partner, recently arrived from Canada. Europe at the end of the twentieth century — with all its material comforts and cultured rituals. At the same time, just two hours by plane from that placid scene, a young man (no less European) was witnessing the destruction of a centuries-old way of life as his former schoolmates and drinking buddies turned on their neighbours with an inexplicable savagery — swiftly putting paid to all those confident high-school history lessons that had taught us 'Never Again in Europe!'

Kemal Pervanic is a thirty-one-year-old Bosnian refugee who arrived in the United Kingdom at the beginning of 1993. He had survived almost seven months of brutality, terror and hunger in Omarska and Manjaca — two of the prison camps which the then triumphant Bosnian Serb political and military leadership had established in Northern Bosnia. The existence of these squalid, deadly places in Europe's heartland had shocked the Continent for a brief media moment towards the end of that hot summer of 1992. But it is doubtful that many of us have as yet taken the full measure of the damage which these accursed camps and their catalogue of horrors have done to the integrity of our European human rights and humanitarian law traditions. Something crucial to modern European self-perception died at places like Omarska and Srebrenica. As historian Michael Ignatieff has written of the Bosnian conflict, 'no one who was there will ever believe in Europe again ...'

Kemal Pervanic's memoir of his time as an inmate of Omarska and Manjaca is a vital and compelling act of resistance. Resistance against forgetting; resistance against the reduction of any human being to the status of a disposable object; resistance against those who insisted on seeing the war in Bosnia as the inevitable explosion of deeply rooted and implacable ethnic hatreds which could only find resolution in partition and segregation. On one level, what is extraordinary about this book is its very ordinariness. For this is the story of a young man from a village indistinguishable from scores of others which suffered the same lightning-quick dissolution of common life during the first months of the war in 1992. It is written — with remarkable poise and control — by a young man who had never thought of himself as an author or a historian, and who was indeed to become the first person from his village to receive a university degree after his release, resettlement and rehabilitation in Britain.

We have had accounts of various aspects of the Bosnian conflict from foreign journalists, academics, and standard-bearers for the benighted 'international community', frequently with greater or lesser helpings of ego attached. From Bosnia itself, we have had a number of moving and incisive meditations on the war from intellectuals, poets, and home correspondents. Many of these books and articles have been peppered with testimony from the grassroots and from individual victims of appalling human rights violations. But *The Killing Days* is surely one of the few first-hand, comprehensive records yet produced by an ordinary Bosnian citizen who endured a particularly bleak chapter of his country's tragic dismemberment.

With commendable economy and understatement, Kemal Pervanic recalls how thousands of Bosnian Muslims and Croats, and a few dissenting Serbs, were beaten, tortured, starved and murdered at the hands of their captors during those first bloody months of the conflict. Although it is primarily a story of the wholesale destruction of the Bosnian Muslim society of the Prijedor–Kozarac region, Kemal's book is a lament for the violent disappearance of a way of life which transcended what he personally regards as the artificial boundaries of religious or national identity.

First and foremost, Kemal's memoir is a narrative of grief at the loss of fundamental humanity which these camps represented. It is a narrative which does not concern itself with the priorities of nationalists or ethnic purists of any stripe — apart from his evident disgust at their stupidities. Like the poet and journalist Rezak Hukanovic's otherwise very different book about the Omarska nightmare, *The Killing Days* makes plain that while the camps were an integral part of the Bosnian Serb national project, those who carried out its ugly demands with the greatest conviction should be viewed more precisely as individual thugs or gangsters rather than as embodiments of collective identity.

Shakespeare wrote that 'the private wound is the deepest' — a judgement that applies to the fate of the Prijedor–Kozarac region during the summer of 1992 with astonishing accuracy. For in this corner of the country, the ferocity of the maiming and killing which took place in the name of the *Republika Srpska* was often directly related to the intimacy of the tormentor and the tormented. Nothing shocks and chastens more in this book than Kemal's roll call of those with whom he had once attended primary school, drank in some village pub, or chatted in a local barber shop — but who then in an instant were transformed into camp guards or agents of terror. The avenging of imagined slights or wrongs among former neighbours and the settling of old scores between families lent the cruelties of Omarska an especially chilling dimension which *The Killing Days* captures in all its painful detail.

But at the core of this chronicle of seemingly limitless inhumanity, there is also resilience and a streak of very dark comedy. The tenderness and generosity between Kemal and his brother, and their fears for their mother's safety; the quiet dignity of broken men who could not be certain that they would live to see another day; the frantic compilation of improvised recipe collections among inmates struggling to keep some memory of home and family alive; the surreal image of the inmates' half-shaven heads after a power cut brings their mass hair clipping session to a sudden halt — these are as much at the heart of this book as the random acts of violence and the body counts which punctuated each and every day at Omarska.

Kemal even manages to have tremendous fun at the expense of his pompous captors — sending up the absurd paranoia of local chieftains possessed by visions of grand Islamic conspiracies; the comic-book patriotism of the shabby impresario who leads the inmates in enforced choral singing in the camp; and the officer who dreams of a boat built by Muslim slave labour, but whose statelet inconveniently lacks a seacoast. But it is the unforgettable moments of compassion and even creativity in the midst of despair that most distinguish this book — the ingenuity of the artist–craftsmen of Manjaca as they fashion beautiful objects out of bits of wood; the gentle tending of the wounded and the sick in the stinking, overcrowded rooms of Omarska; and most especially, Kemal and his brother parting with their last, carefully hidden Deutschmarks in a futile attempt to ransom a condemned man from hideous, certain death.

Editing this book with Kemal over a three-month period at the end of 1998 has taught me much about the reach of the human spirit. The absence of hatred for his captors or a desire for revenge against those who took everything from him — which is so apparent throughout this book — has been confirmed many times over in our conversations. Kemal's aspirations in writing this book — in a language he scarcely knew six years ago — were never self-consciously literary, but moral. Like Primo Levi, he emerged from his imprisonment determined to tell the truth about what he had known in the grim, unsparing universe of the camps.

One day as we worked together on the book, I asked Kemal what he would say today to some of those former schoolmates who had stood guard over him at Omarska were he to meet them face to face. With startling frankness, he told me that in his darkest moments — when he thinks of those who destroyed his home and his world and the lives of so many relatives and friends — he sometimes imagines what it would be like to murder them in turn. He told me, 'I can actually see myself killing them — I watch myself doing it — and I feel nothing as I prepare to do it, or while I am doing it, or after the killing is done. But then ... I realise that I do not *need* to do this — that I do not *want* to do this — that in doing this, I would lose myself completely — lose everything that I am ... And then, I just feel privileged.'

Words such as these are unflinching in their acknowledgement of the scale of the crime committed and the depth of the sorrow and anger of those who survived. And yet, at the same time, they speak of a readiness to break the cycle of violence, of a capacity to allow ourselves, in Seamus Heaney's words, to '... hope for a great sea-change on the far side of revenge'. Kemal's brave words — his desire for justice rather than vengeance — and the book he has written have certainly left me with at least a fragile hope that Europe might just one day learn something from the legacy of this terrible century. In giving us his story in these pages, it is we who become the privileged ones.

Dr Brian Phillips
Amnesty International

Prologue

I was born in 1968, in a small village called Kevljani, in the Prijedor district of north-western Bosnia — a region better known as Bosnian Krajina. Until the 1992–95 Bosnian conflict began, Prijedor town itself had been a mixture of mainly Muslims and Serbs. Villages in the region had often been all Muslim, Serbian, or Croatian, and this was a reflection of our culture and tradition — not of divisions or ancient hatreds. South-west of Prijedor there had been a large Croatian minority, concentrated mainly around the iron-ore mine in Ljubija. There had also been a small number of villages which represented a blend of different ethnic groups. Trnopolje, for example, had been a mixture of the three main groups, but also of a number of other groups like Germans, Ukrainians and Romas.

Until 1992, all these people had cohabited in peace. For my generation the Second World War amounted to no more than a history lesson. I had learned something from these lessons — or at least I thought I had — but I had never felt that this war was related to me in any way — even though my grandfather had become its victim. I had never viewed the Serbs or Croats with whom I had lived and attended the same school as former or present enemies. They were people just like me. We were people who could not sustain our lives without living and working together. Life was regular. I never thought, or had any need to think of my Serb neighbours as people who belonged to a different ethnic group. It's true that we had different religious beliefs, different customs, but we had many more things in common that kept us together than differences that would keep us apart. 'Ancient hatreds', so often served up to the public in the West as 'the real reason' for this 'primitive Balkan slaughter', never existed.

Kevljani had always been populated by Muslims. I am the youngest of three sons. My parents had been born in the mid-thirties, my father in Kevljani and my mother in a small hamlet called Garibi, near Trnopolje. Like so many generations of Bosnians before him, my father had built his family life around his father — who died nine months after my birth. My father earned our living in the northern republics, Slovenia and Croatia. During my childhood I saw him only for weekends. We owned some land which we worked to raise crops and grow food for cattle, and this helped us to supplement my father's rather modest labourer's salary.

I remember the days of my childhood quite vividly. Before starting school, at the age of seven, I spent my days being surrounded by my brothers and my neighbours. I was growing up in a Muslim village, which was surrounded by Serb villages. When I attended my first school, in my village, I was in a mixed class of Muslim and Serb children. Even though we had different names, came from different villages and had different religious backgrounds, I knew nothing of religious life and couldn't understand why it existed or what its purpose was. We had so much in common: *we were just kids*. We didn't know much about life, but if we liked someone from the class more than others, it wasn't because he or she was a Muslim or a Serb. Outside school — at home or in the village — I was never told to hate Serbs. All my teachers in these first years of school were Christians. As former Yugoslavia[1] was run by the communists whose official policy was to unite all peoples around the country under a slogan of 'Brotherhood and Unity', not many people dared to speak openly of hatred or animosities towards other groups as the punishment would be harsh — often in the form of a prison sentence and hard labour. But none of this diminishes the fact that a great deal of tolerance existed between my villagers and my neighbours. Our fathers worked together. Our mothers went to the same markets together. The same tolerance existed throughout the country. In towns, where the population mix was far greater, mixed marriages were a regular occurrence. In rural areas, this was less so.

One important thing that I remember from those days was shops full of relatively cheap food. The food shortages that happened in Yugoslavia in the 1980s were alien to me.

The first disturbing moments that I can remember occurred a year after President Tito's death. The year was 1981. I was thirteen, and in my fifth grade in Omarska. Political problems surfaced in the autonomous province of Kosovo, in the south of Yugoslavia.

Two years earlier I had started the second part of my primary education in Omarska, a Serbian village four kilometres from my house. During these years of peace, Omarska was known for its

---

1. Former Yugoslavia was a federal state, consisting of six republics (Serbia, Croatia, Bosnia & Herzegovina, Macedonia, Slovenia, and Montenegro) which were based on the ethnicity of their majority populations. The only exception was Bosnia, where all three main ethnic groups (Muslims, Serbs, and Croats) were defined as constituent members of the republic. Yugoslavia also had large minority groups, Hungarians and Albanians for example. Albanians had always been a minority group, even though they outnumbered Slovenians almost two to one.

open cattle market, which took place every Wednesday. Sellers came from all around the region, and buyers sometimes came from places as far away as the Croatian coastal town of Split. The less famous part of this market, a grocery market, where people bought and sold groceries and clothes, was situated just across the fence.

In school I met characters like Milan Milutinovic, who shared the same school desk with me, and Milojica Beric, another Serb classmate. I knew Rade Ritan, a likeable character and a witty salesman who never hesitated to crack a joke at your expense; Drasko Gruban, who only days before the Omarska camp was established had still worked in a grocery shop in Kevljani; Drasko's uncle, Rade Gruban, and his younger son Goran, who in the years preceding the conflict had run their own shop less than a hundred metres from the place where their cousin Drasko worked; and Miroslav Kvocka, Mladen Radic, and Zeljko Meakic, three policemen who worked at the police station which was on the other side of the road, a few metres below the school. I could never imagine that all these men would one day embody my worst fears. Some of their names were to become symbols of terror of the worst kind. In those early days, I was coming face to face with these people on a daily basis, never thinking that one day they would be laughing and I would be hiding from their eyes and their laughter, fearing that they might want my head.

My father was working all around Croatia, wherever his company secured a contract. My eldest brother Asim had just finished his compulsory National Service, and got his second job on the Croatian coast. My other brother Kasim was reaching the age for National Service. It was a very calm period of my life.

Two years later, in 1983, I enrolled in the Electrotechnical School in Prijedor. My classmates this time included Croats, too. In the background, the economic situation in the country was worsening all the time. The communists' 'attempts' to reform the country failed. An older generation of communists was still ruling the country with no apparent signs of nationalism yet. I still didn't view my neighbours and fellow students as Serbs or Croats, but as human beings. Nothing dramatic happened in my life during those four years.

I graduated from Electrotechnical School in June 1987, and six months later, in January 1988, I began my National Service. I was lucky. I was to serve in the north-eastern corner of Bosnia, in the small river port of Brcko. I say I was lucky, as my elder brother Asim had had to go all the way to Montenegro in the south and, travelling on the existing infrastructure, it took him almost twenty-four hours to get home from there. For me, it was just a few hours by bus. Another advantage I had over my brothers was that I served only twelve months — as opposed to Asim's eighteen and Kasim's fifteen.

The first part of my National Service — four months of training for defence purposes — I spent in the artillery, an élite part of the garrison. For the remaining eight months I worked as an administrator for support units in the garrison. During this time, the relationship between soldiers of different ethnic backgrounds remained as good as ever. However, below the surface there was a certain prejudice about soldiers of Albanian nationality. They were thought of as a nation of separatists. I didn't enjoy my army life very much. It was something everyone had to do, and I had to do my share.

During my service, I noticed that prices of food and other products were on a constant rise. It seemed that money notes were changing faster than cigarette prices.

Towards the end of the decade, Serbian film-makers began to recreate 'historical' events. At that time, I didn't see their wider implications. I enjoyed watching films like *Migrations*, *Vuk Karadzic*, and *The Battle of Kosovo Field*. But in later years, I realised that this might have had a psychological impact on Serbian people, especially the uneducated masses who saw them not as a pure entertainment — somebody's personal view of those events — but as their history, a reminder of their hardship under the Ottomans. We Bosnian Muslims again became 'Turks' and 'Balije'. As some sort of extension of this psychological 'experiment', some Bosnian Serbs led by a new, very hairy prima donna called Radovan Karadzic (who came from Montenegro, not Bosnia) started excavating pits that contained the bones of victims massacred by the Croatian fascists known as the *Ustashe* during the Second World War. This really scared me. It was a message to the Serbian people that something dark, something sinister and reminiscent of Second World War atrocities, was to be repeated again. What was the intention behind all of this? There was not a word of Serbian butcheries against the civilian Muslim population in the Drina valley from the same period. It looked like the staging of a plot where all Serbs suffered as historical victims, and they were being told that if they were not on the alert it would happen again. From today's perspective, it seems that the psychological warfare started years before the first bullets were fired. But we non-Serbs didn't see it, or more accurately, we didn't even remotely think that something like it could ever happen. We Muslims knew best that our survival was at stake if Yugoslavia ever fell apart.

The western style of elected democracy was not something with which my countrymen or I were familiar. And then, in April 1990, the first free elections were held in two northern republics, Slovenia and Croatia. For me this all happened too fast. We didn't live in a country accustomed to turbulent changes in politics. We were used to a quiet life, where people had a job for life. Politics didn't excite the wider population. But suddenly, the horses pulling the cart called Yugoslavia started running unbridled. Each horse wanted to pull it his own way. Politics became the dominant force in our lives. Papers, TV screens, street conversations — they were all politics. We, ordinary people, who were always told by the party linesmen what to do and how to do it, who had had no word in running the country, became spectators of this huge political circus. But this was a serious business. Politicians who originally came from the same camp started blaming each other for failures to which each one of them had made his fair contribution. Nobody wanted to recognise his own personal failure. The Slovenians clashed with Slobodan Milosevic, who in turn failed to rally the support of the Croats in his frontal assault on the Slovenians. This was all important, because in their minds, ordinary people had started grouping themselves into different camps — Serbian, Croatian, Slovenian.

Suddenly, some younger men from my village started 'maturing' into politicians. Because Slovenians had expressed their will for independence in an earlier referendum, these men were dreaming of dividing the country into two parts — a 'western part' comprising Slovenia, Croatia, and Bosnia, and which, according to them, was progressive and would in a couple of years become part of the European Community; and an 'eastern part' consisting of the three remaining republics, Serbia, Macedonia, and Montenegro.

I loved my country. I didn't want to live in some small ghetto. I thought that on the higher level things were getting out of hand, and that the only solution to the problem was a military coup. This was not the only time I had had positive thoughts about the army. Following the bloody overthrow of the Ceausescu regime in Romania, and the worsening of the political situation in our country with an ever-increasing speed that was leading us all towards an abyss, I believed that the army was the only force that could prevent the disintegration of the country — which could not take place without bloodshed. Following the referendum for independence in Slovenia, there came the first free, multiparty elections — where the old sort of politicians turned into new-born democrats who fought these elections surfing on the crest of a wave of nationalism. I became worried to say the least.

The Killing Days

I thought this was the time for the army to start acting. Seal all the borders; don't let anybody leave the country; push the existing politicians into retirement; create a very strong centre of power; and keep the country together. I never dreamt that this same force would be used as an instrument that was to inflict deep wounds on me, and at the same time would claim the lives of many other civilians.

As politicians from different republics could not come to a peaceful settlement after months of unsuccessful negotiations, first Croatia and then Slovenia declared independence on 25 June 1991. War broke out in Slovenia but lasted only ten days thanks to Slovenia's homogenous population. Without a significant Serbian minority living there, Milosevic was ready to let them go. On 5 July, the European Community imposed the arms embargo on all parts of Yugoslavia. Milosevic wanted to maintain a strong grip on Croatia, but the newly elected Croatian government had decided to put up resistance, too. The fiercest fighting was in Vukovar, a small town in Eastern Croatia. Meanwhile, the UN imposed an arms embargo on all parts of the country. After three months of shelling, Vukovar fell to the Serbs. Croatian Serbs helped by the JNA (Yugoslav People's Army) controlled one third of Croatia. Following recognition of Slovenia's and Croatia's independence by the member countries of the European Community, the vast JNA machine moved to Bosnia.

In 1991, Serbian Democratic Party (SDS) politicians put themselves forward as Bosnian-Serb leaders. As part of their long-term political objectives they declared several Serb Autonomous Regions (SAOs) — one of which was SAO Bosnian Krajina, where I lived. The authorities in Prijedor refused to take part in this. Following their refusal, local Serbs in Prijedor demanded to split all local government institutions into Serbian and Muslim components. A new 'Green Line' was to divide Prijedor and its citizens in two. In October 1991, Karadzic and his followers established the Serbian National Assembly. This meant that, with this political split, Bosnia could no longer function as one entity. Parliamentary sessions became reminiscent of dark comedies. But in its darkest hour, this comedy was to turn into the bloodiest tragedy. Serb threats were flying everywhere. It was becoming apparent that the Serbian people were 'represented' by a bunch of lunatics who didn't care about us in the least.

Bosnian president Alija Izetbegovic asked the UN to deploy its troops in Bosnia in order to prevent threats of possible bloodshed inside Bosnia, but his request was flatly refused. The EC said that every Yugoslav republic would be recognised as independent on the condition that they first held a referendum on this issue. On 1 March 1992, 64 per cent of the Bosnian population went to the polls. 99 per cent voted for independence. A majority of Serbs boycotted the polls. This was the time when the first roadblocks appeared in the streets of Sarajevo.

It was still possible to escape from the Bosnian cauldron. Mama and Kasim were telling me to cut off my hair and slip quietly out of Bosnia. But I refused. I didn't want to leave them behind. JNA troops were bringing artillery pieces back to Prijedor and positioning them on the hills around Muslim villages.

Once in the camp I was told a funny but true story by an old man. He said that some Serbian soldiers who were still incorporated into the JNA didn't have enough manpower to pull a howitzer up a hill. They called some local Muslims working in the field to help them, and they did. Later on, the same howitzer was used to pound those who had pulled it to its new position.

At the end of March 1992, following a referendum on Bosnian independence, Karadzic and his followers established the Bosnian-Serb Parliament with its seat in Pale — a small ski resort in the mountains above Sarajevo. Immediately after that, they declared the Serbian Republic of Bosnia–Herzegovina. 80,000 well-equipped JNA soldiers and reservists changed their name, and with new insignias they became the Bosnian-Serb army. I knew that we Bosnian Muslims had no armed force to defend us against this killing-machine-in-waiting. As we would say in Bosnia, we were to be 'roasted'.

The Bosnian-Serb army's first conquests took place in the Drina valley, in predominantly Muslim areas lying alongside Serbia. Attacks were co-ordinated with armed forces from Serbia, police forces, and numerous paramilitaries from both sides of the border. This was a pattern which was later to be used all over Bosnia. Many civilians were brutally murdered in these raids. A new term, 'ethnic cleansing', was coined. Serbs opened the first camps; the first Muslim women were raped. Bijeljina, Zvornik, Visegrad, Foca — they all temporarily became part of 'Greater Serbia'. The next Serbian move was to secure a corridor that would run alongside the Sava River, an official border in the north between Bosnia and Croatia. The Serbs needed it in order to connect Serb-controlled Knin in Croatia with Serbia proper, as life in Knin was unsustainable without supplies from Serbia. The planned route was to pass through Bosnian Krajina. We were to be their next target.

Part One

The Attack

1

Finally, Gradiska. To reach the bridge, the column needed to pass through the town centre — swarming with a hostile crowd shouting for our blood. Some spat at the bus windows, others threw stones, and the police made no effort to keep the crowd away from the column. Negotiations were taking place on the bridge, and we had no choice but to wait. Suddenly, the glass on one of the windows of my bus shattered. Somebody from the crowd had fired twice. Fortunately, nobody was hurt. I was amazed when I realised that I felt no fear inside me of being hurt. The first buses started crossing the bridge.

Over the bridge, I spotted the first UN forces deployed in the area. They were from Jordan, and were charged with monitoring any breaches of the ceasefire — signed by Serbs and Croats almost a year before this day. The first signs of dusk appeared, and the column headed deeper into Croatian territory. Along the road were the ruins of what once used to be houses. Several kilometres after crossing the bridge, there was not a single sign of any kind of civilian life around. Jordanian soldiers waved to us from their barracks. I had no emotions. No sadness, no joy. Just vast emptiness inside me. I despised the world I had left behind me. I despised the world I was approaching. I hated the world that let all of this happen. But this hatred was silent. The world I was entering into was not the same world as the one I had known in peacetime. I was being deported from my country. It probably saved my life. But what was my life now anyway? I did not want to die, but I still felt no enthusiasm for the life ahead of me. I guess I was like an animal being released into the wilderness after years of confinement. There was a huge hole in my life.

I felt I had been a coward for not having defended my home and my country, even though I had not been given any such opportunity. I felt I was a different kind of human being after these last seven months. Nothing was going to be the same again.

Close to the line of separation between the Zagreb government forces and the rebel Serbs, another group of buses waited for us. The column finally stopped. We started disembarking from the buses. Crossing the line, we were welcomed by members of the International Committee of the Red Cross (ICRC), who put us onto new buses.

'Good evening.' Those before me greeted the new bus driver with smiles on their faces. I just passed him moving towards one of the back seats. I was in no mood to talk. I was a man in No Man's Land. This is where I wanted to stay. I wanted everybody to go ahead and grab their freedom and leave me alone in this land where there was no need to seek independence from others. I wanted to stay in the land where there were no ambitious administrations that could screw up my life to satisfy their own sick ambitions; the land where there were no profiteers using all possible means just to enrich themselves. I was sick of all the people of this world. Man was the most disgusting creature on

Earth. A blind idiot crushing everything he stepped on without looking back at the damage he had done. For seven long months I had wanted to escape from people. All I wanted was just five minutes on my own.

'Hey, chief. Could we hear some news on the radio?' Somebody wanted to hear news that five minutes later would be an insignificant piece of history.

'Yeah. Sure.'

'They were killing indiscriminately. They tortured and killed thousands of people. Each night there were thirty to forty men murdered.' A familiar voice was giving an interview to reporters on a Croatian radio station.

Words of warning from that good ICRC fellow — that it might be dangerous for those staying behind if we talked to the press — obviously had no meaning for the man being interviewed. He was a free man. Crossing the line, he instantly forgot the world behind. He forgot the men still waiting for their release. Looking quietly through the window, I could only ask myself one last time: 'Will we ever learn?'

Earlier that year, 1992, my village, Old Kevljani, had been just another small and quiet place. On the morning of Thursday, 21 May, everything seemed as usual. It was a very pleasant and sunny spring day.

Around 1.30pm Mama started to prepare lunch. I was hanging around the house and my brother Kasim was somewhere in the village. Suddenly, somebody was running and shouting: 'Two thousand Chetniks are moving north of the village.'[1]

It was the news everyone had been expecting — but hoping

---

1. During the Second World War, the Chetniks were Serbian paramilitary troops led by a royalist supporter and Serbian nationalist Draza Mihailovic. They collaborated with Germans and committed horrendous crimes against non-Serbs in Bosnia. After Serbia's attacks on Croatia (1991) and Bosnia (1992) all Serbian irregulars were referred to as Chetniks.

would never reach our ears. The place where the Chetniks had been reported was to the north, about one kilometre away from my house. It was not possible to see them from my place as a thick layer of woods concealed them from sight.

For the last two months, on the face of it, life in the region had seemed normal. But in reality we could all feel the signs of coming trouble. My village was quieter than usual. There was something unpleasant about the quietness. I could not hear people calling each other to leave their gardening and come for a cup of coffee. The biggest sign of change was that there was no noise of children playing. The village was completely silenced. It was not normal for a place like Kevljani to be so quiet.

In better times, the population of Old Kevljani had numbered around six hundred. The village was set between the railway line to the south and the Prijedor–Banja Luka highway to the north. We were the most eastern Muslim village in the Prijedor district, situated at the edge of the territory populated predominantly by the Serbs. We were surrounded by Serbs on three sides. The only direct route leading to Kozarac, the largest Muslim town in the region, was a road running north-east towards the highway. All other routes led directly to Serb villages.

All the houses in the village, about one hundred of them, were lined along three main roads which met in the village centre. I lived with my parents and two older brothers in the central part of the village called *Srednja Mahala*. Mama, Kasim and I were still at home, while my father and elder brother worked in Zagreb, the Croatian capital. Serbian attacks on towns in northern Bosnia and Bosnian Posavina had closed all routes for their safe return.

Kasim had worked in Croatia, too, but several months earlier he had decided to quit and come home. As for myself, like many other young people of my generation, for the last three years I was caught in a widespread trap of unemployment. Some people had decided not to wait and see whether the Serbs would carry out their threats. Instead, they packed their bags and left the village.

Once I heard the news of the Serbs' approach, I ran to the woods above our house. When I arrived there, I heard some voices coming from behind the bushes. Looking very carefully in that direction, I recognised two of my neighbours. They had heard the same news and had also decided to come and investigate for themselves. We remained hidden in the green part of the woods where nobody from the other side could see us. Beyond the woods there was a vast clear area of farmland, and we could see some figures moving along a road at its far end. They were some four to five hundred metres away. From this distance it was impossible to recognise faces. The pair of binoculars I had was of very little help. I could only see their automatic weapons and the olive-green JNA (Yugoslav People's Army) uniforms. They did not try to hide. I had a feeling they wanted to show us who was controlling the whole situation. Behind them there was a forest, and it was possible more of them could have been hiding there.

Some three kilometres further east was the main Serb stronghold of Omarska, and my neighbours decided to move on to the part of the woods facing it to see if there were other Serbs coming from that direction.

'You stay here,' they said. 'More men should join you soon.'

Waiting for others to arrive, I wondered if there was a way we could defend ourselves. Most of us had gone through a compulsory period of National Service, where we had been given some basic training in handling infantry arms such as Kalashnikovs or semi-automatic rifles. But we had not been trained for a conflict of this nature. We had no arms — not even rifles — nor any kind of military organisation. We were just a bunch of villagers at a loss as to what to do. The Serbs had always dominated the JNA and they had appropriated the JNA's small and heavy weaponry.[2]

During the previous couple of days, the village had been preparing to send women and children to Kozarac in case of an emergency. While I was on my way to the woods, our neighbour Hasnija came to our house and told Mama that women, children, and the elderly were being evacuated. In all this panic and confusion, Kasim told her to leave the village immediately. Hugging him in tears, she said: 'My dear son, are we ever going to see each other again?'

As Mama was leaving for the village centre, Kasim remembered that I had some money with me. It was always with one of us in case we had to run. He thought it might be of greater help to her than to the two of us. He ran to the woods to take it from me, but by the time he was back in the village she was already gone. She had had just enough time to put her shoes on. Minutes later, Kasim was back in the woods. The whole family was dispersed now. Two of us were still in the village. Mama was in Kozarac not knowing where she was going to spend the coming night; and my elder brother and father were in Zagreb — which seemed to be on another planet.

---

2. JNA (Yugoslav People's Army) grew out of the Partisan Movement organised and led by Tito and his communist comrades during the Second World War. After World War II, JNA became one of the largest armed forces in Europe. Contributions to JNA's budget came from the pockets of all Yugoslav citizens, but the army structure remained largely disproportionate. Officer corps had more that eighty per cent of Serb nationals. Top of the army had even more than eighty per cent of Serb Generals. In 1991 Serbian forces attacked Croatia with JNA weapons. The Croats were killed by their own weapons, whose production and purchase they financed for forty-six years. The same happened during Serbia's aggression on Bosnia–Herzegovina.

The Yugoslav concept of self-defence also included forces of Territorial Defence. They were run by local governments, and they had their own arms. However, when the Serbian leadership was planning invasions of Croatia and Bosnia, JNA leadership was instructed to take control of all the weapons that belonged to the Territorial Defence. This left the Bosnian Muslims to defend themselves with almost bare hands, against eighty thousand well-equipped and well-trained Serb soldiers. Purchase of arms was not possible because of the arms embargo imposed by the UN on all former Yugoslav republics.

When Serbia attacked Croatia almost all non-Serb officers left JNA. JNA continued to claim its all-Yugoslav character whilst it openly fought for the Serbian cause.

Meanwhile, three more young neighbours arrived in the woods, too. They said several other groups had taken positions at other places around the village.

'I will stay here with them. You go home and feed the animals,' Kasim said to me. 'They haven't been given any food since morning.'

I left them observing the movements of the Serbs through binoculars. Using the longer path home, I passed by the other groups our neighbours had mentioned. I wanted to know how long they intended to stay there. All of them told me they were going to guard the village during the coming night from their present positions.

Back home everything looked so sad. In the kitchen there was a pie covered by a tray that Mama had made just before she fled. It was still warm. Next to it were some freshly roasted coffee beans. The house looked ghostly, as if suddenly all life had disappeared without a trace. Barking dogs were the only sounds that could be heard in the village. I fed the animals and gave them some water. Halfway through the job, I noticed a small group of the villagers I had left behind in the woods coming back to Kevljani.

'Why are you coming back?' I asked. 'Weren't you supposed to stay there all night?' I wondered what had made them change their minds so suddenly.

'It's not too safe to stay there in the dark,' they said. 'We don't have enough weapons to defend ourselves if the Chetniks decided to attack tonight.'

'Well,' I thought, 'it doesn't really matter whether they attack by day or by night. Whichever they do we have no weapons to stop them.' Nevertheless, I thought these men should have remained in the woods — if only to alert everybody in the village.

I went back inside the house to get something to eat. Soon, Kasim came back home, too.

'What would you like to eat?' I expected him to be hungry as he had not eaten anything for some seven or eight hours.

'I'm not hungry,' he replied.

'What are you going to do tonight?'

'We're going to watch all the approaches to the village closely.'

'Should I go, too?'

'It would be better for you to stay at home, and when I get tired around midnight you can replace me until morning.'

The rest of the night went by without any incidents. After the excitement of the previous day and a sleepless night, everyone fell asleep the following morning. Nobody thought that the Serbs would begin their attack at first daylight. Fortunately, the morning passed quietly.

The problems that we, the Muslims of the Kozarac region, were facing were also well known to the Muslims of Brdo — a group of villages set on the western side of Prijedor town. Since the Serbs had ousted Prijedor's legally elected government some weeks earlier, they now demanded that the non-Serb populations accept their rule. Both we, the Muslims of the Kozarac region, and those from Brdo, rejected such an option because we knew what had happened to the Muslims in the Drina Valley — where some people were massacred and others expelled. After the coup in Prijedor, no-one could trust the Chetniks.[3]

---

3. Since the start of Serbia's agression on Croatia in 1991 Prijedor became the new 'wild west'. Soldiers with rifles on their shoulders were a daily sight in Prijedor's streets. Local government had no powers to do anything about it. Soldiers brandished their weapons, discharging rounds of ammunition, when in a 'good mood'. While the Muslims and the Croats refused to join the Serbs in their conquests in Croatia, the Serbs were preparing the ground to change the Prijedor government by force. They organised several illegal police stations with more than a thousand men armed by JNA. Apart from arming illegal police units JNA delivered arms to the entire local Serb population. Very often deliveries were supplied by army helicopters that landed in Serbian villages in broad daylight.

Led by Simo Drljaca the illegal Serbian police overthrew Prijedor's government on April 30. They encountered no resistance. Armed men were positioned at all key positions in the town. Snipers were placed in the town hall, the police headquarters, the communications centre, the law courts buildings, and the post office. Teachers, doctors, managers, judges, and all non-Serb employees in local companies were dismissed from their working places. The new 'government' frequently used Radio Prijedor to issue ultimatums to non-Serbs to surrender all arms. They demanded that the police

The Attack

While we rested in our village after the sleepless night, on the other side of Prijedor five uniformed Serbs in a vehicle were approaching the checkpoint controlled by Muslims from Hambarine — a village in Brdo. The checkpoint had been established out of fear that the Serbs might enter the village and massacre the people. The five men demanded to be let through. They were told to drive back to where they came from. One of them, thinking that the machine gun would be a better method of persuasion, walked back to the vehicle, took up his gun and blasted fire at the men standing at the checkpoint. They fired back and shot him dead. Two more Chetniks died instantly and two were wounded. The dead body of the unsuccessful negotiator was placed in the vehicle and one of the wounded irregulars drove back towards Prijedor.

In the evening, the Serbs used the radio station in Prijedor to broadcast another ultimatum to the Muslims of Hambarine. They named Aziz Aliskovic, a former policeman, and a group of other men, demanding their surrender by 7.00am the following morning. None of the men they asked for were present at the checkpoint at the time of the incident. The ultimatum was not met.

The Serb-controlled television station, TV Banja Luka,

---

in Kozarac (almost one hundred per cent a Muslim place) disarm their people and that a Serbian flag must fly in Kozarac. Transmitting these ultimatums on radio waves was the best way to inflame the Serbian population against their Muslim and Croat neighbours. The Serb leaders knew that the arms we had were few and far between, and that once they were ready to attack we could not stand in their way.

Before the coup the Serbs had already taken over the Lisina TV transmitter on the Kozara Mountain. The only pictures we could receive came from the Serb-controlled TV Banja Luka and TV Belgrade, which bombarded us daily with poisonous propaganda. Its effects were immediate. A few days after the coup an armed Serb killed four Muslims outside Prijedor. First he took two passengers, a mother and her daughter, from a bus heading for Prijedor, and he shot them. Then he stopped two men from Brezicani, Jusuf Kuckovic and his neighbour, who were transporting hay on a tractor trailer, and he shot them too. He never answered for his crimes. He was never investigated or prosecuted. The Serbs assumed the role of sharpshooters, and as for the Bosnian native 'Indians' — only dead Muslims were good Muslims. New Prijedor's sheriff, Simo Drljaca, thought we Indians had no right to complain.

presented a completely different version of the event. One of the wounded irregulars told the TV cameras that he and his colleagues were simply going home from the front in Croatia. The Serbian propaganda had transformed this incident into a deadly plot against all the Serbs by Muslim extremists. The same TV station was used as a vehicle for propaganda which presented the Serbs as being under threat from the Muslims wherever they moved.

When the demands for the delivery of Aziz and the others had not been met, the deadline was extended until 9.00am. Two hours later, the silence in Hambarine was broken by two shells landing on the village. It was a warning. The people of Hambarine decided to remain firm in their decision not to deliver a single man. They knew that the casualties at the checkpoint were the result of self-defence, and that the men the Chetniks demanded had not been there at the time of the incident. At 10.30am, the village came under heavy shell fire. Weapons used for the attack were stationed at the aerodrome at Urije, a suburb of Prijedor. The shell fire was followed by an infantry attempt to overrun Hambarine, but the defenders succeeded in driving them back. The first attempt to capture Hambarine ended in failure. The second try followed soon, but once more the Chetniks were forced to retreat. They resumed heavy shelling. Ground skirmishes lasted until 7.00pm.

Entering Hambarine with two tanks and an armoured personnel carrier (APC), the Chetniks forced the locals to withdraw to nearby Kurevo and Ljubija. Some five hundred people, all unarmed civilians, were never given the chance to run for cover. They became the victims of the first mass slaughter in the district.

2

In the days that followed, the situation in my village had calmed down somewhat. Some of those evacuated to Kozarac did not believe that we would be attacked at all, and had decided to return back home. Twenty-four-hour guards were posted at the approaches to the village to make sure that we would not be taken completely by surprise should the Serbs decide to attack.

Since Mama left, I could not manage to milk the cows and the goats. I tried but I lacked the skill. My neighbour Fadila helped me out for a day or two. When she left with her children too, it fell to her husband Emir to do the job. Unlike me, he had mastered these skills some years earlier — having had to take on the milking after the death of his mother.

On Sunday morning, 24 May, I was in my house with Emir and Armin. For a year or two since Emir had been made redundant, we had spent a lot of time together. Armin was three years younger than me, and we grew up in the same neighbourhood. He was Emir's brother-in-law. This morning we ignored the reality. We joked while having coffee. At lunchtime I started cooking a meal. Emir proved to be of great help. He even baked *pogaca* for Kasim and me, a traditional Bosnian home-made bread. I wished I was able to do all these jobs, as it would have helped me greatly at this time. I felt Emir was very lucky for knowing how to do them.

At 2.00pm, the pleasant atmosphere inside the house was interrupted by sudden gunfire. This was not accidental gunfire caused by the mishandling of a weapon. It was constant and came from a heavy machine-gun. All three of us realised it was taking place on the highway in Gornji Jakupovici. With every second it was rising in intensity. Machine-gun fire was soon accompanied by tank shells. Emir quickly jumped up and went straight home to put on some warm clothes. It was a very warm spring day, and we were lightly dressed. He was wearing only shorts and a T-shirt. If we had to leave the village, he wanted to be dressed properly. Millions of thoughts rushed through my head. All the threats issued earlier by the Chetniks were suddenly coming true. It was no longer fire in Hambarine, some twenty kilometres away. It was right here. It was happening in my own village. Attacks that had killed thousands of Muslims in Bijeljina, Zvornik, Bosanski Brod, and Visegrad had now reached our own homes.

When the first shots were fired that afternoon, Kasim was in the woods. Those staying with him soon left to check out another part of the woods. After twenty minutes, they returned to the village. We were not soldiers; we had no instinct for strategy; and it was therefore impossible for us to organise ourselves efficiently. Armin and I ran to the woods when we learned that no-one had informed Kasim about their withdrawal. When we got there, we found him lying in the bushes on the edge of the woods, observing movements on the road across the plain. He had decided to remain there after spotting several armed Chetniks. The intensity of the fire in Gornji Jakupovici was still increasing. Armin and I suggested we should withdraw into the village, but Kasim refused. We explained that nobody else had remained in the woods, insisting that there was a strong possibility of the first shells landing directly in the area in which we found ourselves. So we all left the woods and returned to Kevljani.

The people in the village were in a panic. No one knew what to do. Soon after we returned, the first shells started to fly above our heads, piercing the air above the village. The brisk noise of flying shells made me very uncomfortable. Coming from the Serbian village of Janjici, some two kilometres north of Kevljani, they were landing in the central part of the village at close intervals. I had a feeling our attackers were only adjusting their weapons for more precise shelling in the coming night.

The first shells targeted the village mosque. With the minaret rising thirty metres above the ground, it was visible from all approaches to the village. None of the shells hit it directly, but they did cause damage to a couple of the surrounding houses, and some landed in the mosque graveyard.

A couple of weeks earlier, it had been decided that in the event of an attack all the villagers should withdraw to a safer place — a small wood near the river. By 5.00pm almost everyone had left the village. The only signs of life in our neighbourhood were several voices coming from Serif Pervanic's front yard, some two hundred metres away. Between shellings Kasim, Armin and I ran from our house to the village centre. Adem Udovcic's house stood close to the mosque, and from there we had a good view of anyone coming towards it from three different sides. The front door was locked so we decided to break it down. Ten to fifteen minutes later, we noticed Emir walking in our direction. We called him and he joined us inside the house. This time he was wearing a winter jacket and carrying a big bag.

Soon afterwards, another familiar figure appeared on the road. A young boy, Edo, was strolling as if nothing unusual was happening around us. Almost laughing, I asked him: 'Do you know what's going on in the village? Where are the people?'

'There are only a few left here,' he said. 'Everybody else has already gone towards the river.'

A few men were still at Serif's place. If they were to join the others soon, we expected them to come our way. We decided to wait for them. During the next hour nobody arrived.

Meanwhile Emir decided to go towards the river on his own. Believing the men at Serif's place were still in the village, Kasim wanted Armin and me to leave while he stayed alone to wait for them. We wanted him to come with us but he refused.

Armin and I ran from house to house. Sensing that another wave of shells was going to land, we stayed under cover for ten to fifteen minutes and had a cigarette. By the time we joined the rest of the villagers, we realised that there had been a change in plans. Instead of the woods, the river had been chosen as a shelter. Its banks were high and steep. Coming up the river bank, our next door neighbour Dido asked: 'Why didn't you join everybody else earlier?'

'There is another group of men at Serif's place. We were waiting for them to come by Adem's house.'

'But they have been here for some time.' He surprised us. They had crossed Baretci (the plains below Adem's house) instead of coming by road.

We had not expected them to take this route as it would make them easier targets for the Serbs' guns. Using the road seemed more logical to us, as the rows of houses on both sides offered far better protection.

'Where is Kasim?'

'He's still in Adem's house.' Dido and Asim Hodza left for the village to find him.

Armin and I descended to the river. The water in this part of the river was shallow. Somewhere further up the stream had been redirected to one of the large water reservoirs which were the main source of water for the local villages. The flat bottom part of the bank, from where the water had receded, was jam-packed with men, women, and children — some were elderly; some were still babies only a few months old. It offered better protection than the nearby woods which, being on the open ground, were more widely exposed to the shells and gunfire.

Half an hour later Dido, Asim and Kasim joined the rest of us. Several hours had passed since the first shells had landed in the village. The sun was setting and everyone was filled with anxiety over what might happen during the coming night.

With the first signs of dusk, the shelling resumed. The shells flying above our heads became more frequent. Around 8.00pm, after a short break, I expected a new wave of shells. But all I could hear were three or four individual shots being fired from a semi-automatic rifle. Suddenly, fire from thousands of rifles and from anti-aircraft machine guns was coming from all directions. Branches of trees on both sides of the river were shattered and scattered by the gunfire. The river's banks were more than two metres high, giving us adequate protection, but the firing seemed to be getting closer. Many different thoughts rushed through my head with incredible speed. My stomach turned upside down.

'Is this it? Is this how life finishes, with my heart trying to jump out of my chest?' I wondered.

Some people looked paralysed. They just sat with their legs deep in the water. They seemed not to be breathing at all. A young boy lying next to me was shivering uncontrollably. Others panicked, shouting: 'They're coming! They'll kill us all!'

'No they're not.' Somebody tried to calm them down. 'They wouldn't dare to come by night.' Dogs with their tails between their legs were trying to hide under crouching people. Their whimpering sounded like small children crying.

'They are getting closer!' Said Velic shouted. 'Let's go out and defend ourselves!' Brandy seemed to have boosted his confidence.

'They are not coming. The night is bright and that only makes it seem as if they were coming.' Mustafa Pervanic was amongst those who remained calm.

'You don't have to go. But I'm going.' Said tried to leave the river bed. Those closer to him grabbed him, trying to take his gun. Finally, he calmed down a bit.

A thought kept crossing my mind: 'Is Mama still in Kozarac? Is she still safe? Kozarac itself is under fire.'

A few moments of silence. Then the shelling started again. Kasim counted the shells. Around midnight he counted as many as four hundred before stopping.

In the short lulls between shellings, all sorts of suggestions were flying around.

'Let's go inside those houses,' said my friend Noko and a few others. 'It's safer in there.'

'We should stay where we are,' others insisted.

'But it's no longer safe here. If a single shell hits us there will be many dead and wounded.' After a few minutes of arguing, those advocating a move to the houses left.

'Maybe they will stop the fire if we talk to them.' Medo Hadzic suggested that establishing a contact with our Serb friends and neighbours in Radivojci might help. But the people were disoriented. They seemed unable to decide whether this was a good suggestion or not.

'Are you sure they will want to talk to you?' somebody asked.

'I have Milenko Kobas's phone number,' Medo continued. 'I'll call him and say we want to surrender.' Medo, his brother Ilijaz, and Sero Velic left, but returned shortly afterwards.

'What happened? Did you talk to anyone?' A glimmer of hope

appeared in everyone's eyes.

'I tried several times,' Medo said. 'The phone was ringing but nobody picked it up.'

'What are we going to do? We can't stay here all night.'

'Perhaps we should try to sneak through their lines and get to Kozarac.' A new suggestion.

'What about the women and children? And the road leading to Kenjari has been blocked for several days. The Chetniks from Petrov Gaj put several machine-guns there. It would be impossible for a bird to fly through.'

'We should definitely not stay here. This is the worst possible place to spend the rest of the night.' Muhamed, Serif's oldest son, thought it would be best to go back to our homes. His father Serif had not come to the river. He had stayed at home and Muhamed had just been back to the village to check if his father was all right. 'We should use the next break and go back. They are not going to enter the village tonight.'

A few still believed that shells would keep missing the part of the river in which we were crammed. 'It's best to stay here and wait until morning,' they said. But they had no idea what we should do when morning came.

'Mortars can't get through walls. If we stay here we'll get killed,' Muhamed appealed, one last time. In the end, we stayed in the river. Shelling and gunfire alternated until five o'clock in the morning.

3

In the morning, when the firing stopped, we needed to decide quickly what to do next. It was far too dangerous to stay around the river and wait for the Chetniks to come. We needed to try and establish some kind of contact with them. An agreement was reached that a delegation consisting of Sero, Ilijaz, Noko and Asim should go to the local primary school in the hope of finding the Chetniks there, in order to try and negotiate the terms of our surrender. Somebody brought a white bed sheet from a nearby house, which Sero and Noko put on a piece of fallen branch to indicate to the Chetniks that they wanted to talk. When they reached the part of the road between the school and a grocery shop, no one seemed to be there. They called out the names of some of the men from Radivojci they knew well, but nobody replied. In a dilemma as to what to do next, they suddenly saw several Chetniks stand up from behind the school's fence.

'Raise your hands,' they commanded.

'We came to talk.' Raising their hands, they tried to explain why they were there, but the Chetniks were not in the mood for talking. They were pushed against the school wall and searched.

'Now I'm going to kill every one of you,' threatened one of the Chetniks they did not know. Moments later, the commander, Momcilo Radanovic — a former taxi driver from Omarska better known by his nickname, Cigo — arrived and yelled at his men: 'Leave them alone!' He listened to our delegation, who told him that we wanted to surrender. Cigo gave them his terms. He wanted everybody, with or without arms, to come to the school at 10.45am. Sero, Ilijaz and Noko came back to tell us this. Asim stayed there. No one knew why.

At least now we knew that the shelling had definitely stopped, so we could come out into the open. The wood where we had originally planned to take refuge was destroyed. We all gathered on the road next to the local electricity distribution station.

While I was talking to Damir, my ex-schoolmate, we heard something whistling above our heads. We realised it was the sound of bullets. It became clear that they were coming from Tadici, a nearby small group of Serbian houses. We quickly moved out of the sniper's sight and hid behind some houses.

When it was almost time to go to the school I realised that we might be searched, in which case I could kiss the money I kept in my pocket goodbye. I was thinking quickly what I should do with it. Kasim suggested I should ask one of the older and most respected women, Smaila, to hide it for me, as it was unlikely that the Chetniks would search the women. I asked her son Ramo if she could possibly do this for me.

'It'd be better if you asked somebody else,' he said. He was concerned about her safety if women were to be searched, too. I understood this concern and I told Kasim I was going to bury it somewhere. Time was running out.

'Hurry up,' Kasim said. I went back to the river and buried the money beneath the roots of an old willow tree on the river bank. The main group had already left and the only way to catch up with them was to cross the meadows. There was a wonderful smell of wild flowers. But in the deep grass there were hidden craters and unexploded shells, so I had to tread very carefully.

I managed to catch up with the last group of people from Kevljani. The Chetniks at the school wore olive-green JNA uniforms with white ribbons on their shoulders.[4] Some were cleanly shaven and had short haircuts. Others had wild long hair, beards and moustaches. Most of the faces came from the surrounding Serb villages, Maricka, Jelicka, Petrov Gaj, Gradina, Omarska, and Gornja Lamovita. But others were strangers speaking with an accent that could only be from some part of Serbia or Montenegro. Many of the local Chetniks were people who had gone to school with us, and with whom we socialised regularly. At the gate to the football pitch, we were searched. Most women and children were allowed to pass without harassment. A Chetnik who was searching the men leered at one of the women and wanted to 'search' her. Another standing next to him stopped him. He himself continued to search the men, while letting this woman and all the others behind her through the gate. A third Chetnik, a stranger with a long black moustache and beard, and without several front teeth, wanted to know if anyone was wounded. His accent indicated he was from Serbia. Finding that nobody was wounded he swore at us, 'You motherfuckers! So we shelled all night without harming anybody? All those shells were used for nothing.' His eyes were full of hatred and looked as deadly as his weapons.

'Why did you shell us with mortars all night?' the Chetniks

---

4. During the Serb aggression on Croatia, armed groups on both sides wore the same uniforms. To distinguish a friend from an enemy, they had to wear ribbons, changing the colour every day. When the Serb army returned to Bosnia they brought this practice with them.

then demanded.

'What mortars?' We were mystified.

'What mortars? Where did all those mortar shells that landed in Radivojci come from?'

We wondered if it was possible that some of their shells really had landed in Radivojci. 'We had no mortars. It could only have been your men stationed at the railway line,' we said.

'And the barrage of rifle fire? I suppose that wasn't you either?' It finally dawned on us that he was being sarcastic.

At the football pitch, we were ordered to sit on the ground. The house across the road belonged to a Muslim doctor from Tuzla, who spent a part of his holidays here every summer. The windows had been blown out. It had obviously been hit by an anti-tank missile. Part of the school roof was burnt, too. All the windows on the village hall were broken. Obviously the Chetniks fired at the buildings first and then searched them, unaware that all the buildings were empty before their arrival.

Most of the Chetniks guarding the football pitch kept their distance, but two came over and asked: 'Why did you need all of this? Why didn't you join us in the fight against the *Ustashe*?[5] Did you have to vote for Alija Izetbegovic and independent Bosnia? Wouldn't it have been better for all of you to live together with us in the new Yugoslavia? We went to school together. My children and his children' — he pointed at me — 'could have done the same.' I kept my head down, thinking, 'Thank God I'm not married. Thank God I have no children.'

Both of them had obviously been drinking. They did not

---

5. During World War II, *Ustashe* were Croatian nationalists — members of the special forces (an equivalent of the SS troops) within the Croatian Army. The head of NDH (Independent State of Croatia), a German puppet-state that existed from 1941-45 and included most of Croatia and the whole of Bosnia, pursued a genocidal policy of ethnic cleansing, mainly against the Serbs. *Ustashe* were executors of this policy. Following 1990's democratic elections, the Serbs started labelling the new Croatian government as reawakened *Ustashe*, as enemies of all the Serbs.

sound angry and abusive. The one with the ginger beard offered some cognac to the men sitting before him. They thanked him but refused to take it.

'Don't worry,' he said, 'have some. I have another bottle anyway.'

'Magic potion for brave warriors,' I thought.

Not very long afterwards, we were all gathered on the pitch when the local Serb civilians, our neighbours, started appearing behind surrounding hedges. They all carried Kalashnikovs. Obviously they had long been armed and were well prepared for all of this. Yet the previous Thursday evening some of us had been with them in the village hall, having a cup of coffee and a chat — agreeing that the current situation was some kind of misunderstanding between 'our leaders', and that everything would be resolved very soon. These same guys now kept their distance from us as if we were lepers. Some time ago one of them, Zune, had had a machete made by a blacksmith from my village. He had used it to cut big pumpkins with which he fed his farm animals. Zune brandished the machete jokingly and exclaimed: 'A war trophy!'

'Nonsense. You know who made it and what it was made for,' said Zune's friends who were sitting amongst us.

We were given some water they brought from the school's well. Several children were given some fruit juice which came from the local shop that the Chetniks had broken into and plundered the day before. Some older women and weaker children were fed bean soup. But this was all a set-up for the TV cameras.

A crew from TV Banja Luka arrived. Two Chetniks, Zeljko Romanic and Milenko Valaula, posed for the cameras. They showed the machete and Zeljko said, 'This is what these Turkish motherfuckers were going to use on my children.'

Sero Velic was picked to speak for the cameras as our representative. They told him what to say — which was to praise the army for their kindness.

In the meantime Serif Pervanic, the most influential man in the village, was still at home. He had not taken refuge with us in the river bed, and so was still unaware of the situation in which we found ourselves. Cigo sent somebody to the village to tell him to come to the school. He came and was sitting on a chair opposite us when a Chetnik guard exclaimed: 'Who are you to sit here and not there with others? Are you *Ustasha*?'

'I am not.'

'We should kill you anyway.' He kept up this harassment until Cigo arrived. Serif and Cigo knew each other very well. They shook hands.

'Serif, what was that last night?'

'What do you mean?' Serif asked in confusion.

'You know. You fired at us and shelled us.'

'Nobody fired at you. You fired at us.'

'No, no. You fired first and we just fired back. It was defence.'

'I guarantee we didn't fire at you.'

'My soldiers are like my own sons,' Cigo said. 'Two of them are dead. They survived eight months of fighting in Croatia just to come back and die at home.'

These two soldiers had died the day before in Gornji Jakupovici. Cigo, of course, did not mention the massacre of the people in Jakupovici — most of whom were only seventeen or eighteen years old. Only a handful of Jakupovici's male population had survived.

Turning his back to Serif, Cigo asked us, 'Is everyone from the village here?' He wanted to know if someone was missing.

'Yes.'

'Have you surrendered all the arms?'

'Yes, we have. They are all in the pile at the village hall.'

'Is that all you had? And where are the remaining four

hundred?'

'Here we go again,' I thought.

'Four hundred what?' Everyone was puzzled. Every child, woman and old man would have had to carry two guns each, as all together we numbered less than two hundred. They could not believe that the whole of Kevljani had only four Kalashnikovs (privately bought from their own soldiers on the black market, by the way), plus some hunting guns, a few legally owned pistols, and a few home-made weapons.

'Where is the special anti-tank unit? And the sniper unit — the hundred and fifty snipers?'

'I don't believe this,' I thought, 'this can't be real.' At that moment we heard a couple of sniper shots. As if the sniper knew Cigo was demanding a hundred and fifty of them.

'Here it is,' he said, 'this is your sniper fire.' We knew we had no snipers and there was nobody left in the village. Zido stood up, saying indignantly: 'This can only be coming from Tadici.' One of our women (who was married to a Serb) quickly said: 'It's Avdo Velic shooting.' She had not noticed Avdo sitting just a few metres away from her. He stood up and said: 'I am Avdo Velic.'

'What are they going to accuse us of next?' I wondered.

Three men from Kenjari arrived. I recognised Rifet Pidic, son-in-law of Serif Pervanic. I was not familiar with the other two men. They wanted to negotiate the surrender of their village. They were told to surrender all their arms unconditionally, if they wanted to avoid the fate that had befallen us the previous night. While this 'negotiating' was going on, we could still hear guns and shells targeting Kozarac.

'You have two hours to come back with your decision. If you fail, we'll attack.' Cigo had nothing more to say to them.

'We'll be back by 5.00pm.' The three men left. They had to hurry up if they were to meet the deadline set for their surrender. It was going to take them at least forty minutes to get to Kenjari, and then another forty minutes to come back. They had no more than forty minutes to persuade their men to surrender.

As the men from Kenjari left, we had to choose several men from our group, each of whom would go with a group of Chetniks to check every house in the village in order to determine that they were truly empty. Cigo led the military police to the surrendered pistols. A kind of a fight broke out.

'I want this one.'

'No, no, I want that one. You can take the other one.' The rest of the weaponry was loaded in the boot of the military police car. Cigo had said to us earlier: 'Nothing is going to happen to you. Those of you with a clean licence of ownership will get your guns as soon as you are released.' The guns that ended up on the belts of the military police all had a clean licence of ownership.

Minutes later the search parties left for our village. Two APCs [Army Personnel Carriers] and a tank remained behind. Cigo pulled a list out of his shirt pocket. As he stood quite close to me I could see there were some pictures and names on the list.

'Listen everyone. I am going to call out some names. If you hear your name, stand up.' Anxious whispers started spreading on the ground.

'Muhamed (Hasan) Velic, Nijaz (Meho) Sivac, Ilijaz (Smail) Hadcic ...' I felt the blood in my veins turn to ice. Most of these men earned their living working in Croatia. I believed Kasim would be on the list, too, since he had worked there for several years before quitting his job. I saw that the same thought had also occurred to Kasim. Fortunately, he was not on the list. It was a huge relief. I felt compassion for the guys who were on it. Several of those on the list were not present. They were still working in Croatia. Those present were taken behind the school and brutally beaten. We heard sounds of blunt objects hitting bodies, cries of pain and the Chetniks' swearing. On the football pitch, everyone was silent. The men they were beating were then taken to a

schoolroom directly in front of us. The windows were wide open. They wanted us to hear what was going on.

We heard grunts, yells, swearing, and the clatter of fallen chairs and tables. Zahid, one of the victims, was ordered to sit in one corner. Giving him a pen and a clean sheet of paper, the Chetniks ordered: 'Write.'

'What about?' Zahid asked in confusion.

'Everything. Everything you know. Who possessed the weapons, who organised the defence.'

'I don't know anything. There is nothing I can write about.'

His hands were shaking so much that even if he had had something to write about he would not have been able to. He later told me that pieces of rubber had been pushed inside their mouths to stop them crying aloud. Blows sent them across the room, knocking down chairs and tables. Blood was spurting across the walls and the floor. Broken teeth were lying all over the floor. Then the Chetniks came out and called more names. They looked crazed and thirsty for fresh blood. We were frightened. The new names made no sense. If it was possession of guns — some of them had not owned guns and none of them had worked in Croatia. Why them? Who was next?

Cigo sent somebody to bring back the Chetniks from our village. The guards who had kept their distance came closer and formed a circle around us. Their arms were ready to fire. Those who had been beaten in the school were loaded on to a small army lorry and taken in the direction of Gornja Lamovita — where the Chetniks supposedly had their base for this operation. The two APCs and the tank followed the lorry.

The rest of us were kept on the football pitch until 5.00pm. The Chetniks who went to check the river where we had spent the previous night came back first. All they found there were a couple of axes and hay forks. They laughed mockingly: 'Were you preparing a peasant rebellion? You can't fight against us. You use guns — we respond with canons. You use canons — we use airplanes. You use airplanes — we use the atomic bomb.' I couldn't imagine where he thought he'd get the last one.

When the three men from Kenjari failed to come back by the deadline, we were told we could go home and that there would be no further attacks on us. Meanwhile, to everybody's surprise, Asim Hodza was approaching from behind a high hedge. We all thought he'd been killed earlier in the morning. The back of his green jacket was torn with a combat knife in the shape of a huge crucifix. The Serbs could have done it for two reasons. First, he was a village *imam* (a local cleric), and second, his jacket was green — the colour associated with Bosnian Muslims. He had arrived from the village of Garibi, where he had been sent with an ultimatum: if they did not also surrender, everybody in our village would be killed. Garibi refused to consider this threat seriously.

Before we left the football ground, Cigo said that mixed patrols would be formed of both our men and his men, to ensure our safety in the coming days and nights. 'If you hear any shell fire tonight do not be afraid. Because Kenjari failed to surrender we will be attacking them tonight.'

Much later, we found out that the force which had made the assault on my tiny village numbered more than a thousand soldiers, surrounding the village from all four sides. Three tanks had entered the village from three different directions, accompanied by APCs equipped with anti-aircraft machine-guns — whose huge bullets could cut a man in two. We were like a group of Bushmen confronting a battalion of the French Foreign Legion.

Back in the village, after our first detention at the school, people went to look for the cattle and horses that they had released at the time of the attack on the previous day. Bilal's house was near the railway line. Between his house and the railway stood some woods and plains, and he thought his cow must have gone into these fields. His neighbour Mesa was looking for his horse, too. Their search led them straight into the Chetniks deployed along the railway line. Both men were in their sixties. Laughing, the Chetniks threatened to hang them on the railway electricity posts. 'Choose the one you like most,' they said.

Mesa was never the kind of person to scare easily. 'Okay,' he said. 'I've tried lots of things in my life but never that. Let's give it a go.'

The Chetniks let him go, but Bilal was taken to the police station in Omarska. He was surprised when he got there to find the men who had been taken from the school. The lorry had left in a different direction. The commander of the police station, Zeljko Meakic, knew Bilal quite well. He offered him some food and some *sljivovica*, a plum brandy. Not daring to refuse, Bilal tried to eat and drink, but his hands shook so much that he could hardly put food in his mouth or lift the glass of *sljivovica*. He described the guys from the village as very quiet and full of fear. They were hardly recognisable. Their faces were deformed by bruising. After brief questioning, Bilal was sent home.

Around noon on the day before the attack, on Saturday 23, another villager, Husein, had been coming back home from Kozarac. Riding his bike on the Prijedor–Banja Luka highway, he was stopped by a group of armed men from Radivojci. They had been surveying this route to Kozarac for some time, but never before had they stopped someone. They knew him. They were our neighbours from Radivojci. He was questioned as to whether he knew anything about armed resistance in our village. He said there was no armed resistance, deeming it dangerous and unnecessary to mention the few people he knew who had guns. He was detained in Radivojci for the next twenty-four hours. When the resistance in Gornji Jakupovici was crushed, he was taken to the Omarska police station for further interrogation. The police wanted to know about a lorry full of weapons that Muhamed Pervanic had, according to them, brought to the village. Muhamed worked as a lorry driver for a Croatian transport company. Sometimes he was able to spend the weekend at home in our village on his way to the place of delivery. Somehow, the Serbs believed that on one of these regular visits home he had brought with him a truckload of armaments.

During the interrogation, one of the policemen went outside. Some minutes later he returned with his arms covered in blood up to his elbows. He addressed Husein with the words: 'If you don't tell us the truth we'll slit your throat.'

Husein was paralysed with fear. He thought the policeman had slaughtered someone outside. It turned out that the policeman had killed a rabbit — whose blood he used to terrify Husein.

Returning to the village from the football pitch, we met two Chetniks carrying bags of coffee beans, and others carrying TV and VCR sets. This made us afraid to go back to what had been home only yesterday. Was it safe to go home? Would they come back to loot our possessions? The prospect of the coming night was dominated by fear.

I did not go home directly. First I went to collect the money I had hidden in the morning. Muhamed, the suspected 'arms dealer', was coming my way. He was looking for his jacket which he'd left on the river bank. We talked about unexploded shells concealed in the thick grass, and the craters created by the explosions.

'This summer I'll have to mow those fields,' he said. 'I'll have to be very careful not to hit the shells.' He had no idea he would never get the chance to mow those fields. He was killed shortly afterwards, together with his father, Serif, and these were the last words I ever heard him say.

The Attack

At Meho Velic's house, I found Emir feeding Meho's cattle and horses. I stopped and helped him. Shortly afterwards, Meho himself arrived. He looked very worried. His brother Hamed was amongst those taken away by the Chetniks.

'I don't believe Hamed will stay alive,' he said. He shook his head in disbelief and sighed deeply.

'Of course he will,' Emir and I tried to comfort him, 'he's done nothing wrong. He didn't even possess a gun. There's no reason for the Chetniks to kill him.'

We went for a cup of coffee at Emir's house. After the tension and the fright of the last twenty-seven hours, the wonderful smell of freshly brewed coffee was like balm to our frayed nerves. I was totally worn out, both physically and mentally. Drinking the coffee slowly, I was thinking how nice it would be to relax and have a long hot bath. This quiet atmosphere was interrupted by Kasim. As I had not yet been at home, he had got worried and was looking for me. We left Emir and Meho sitting in silence and went home.

Back at home, I tried to prepare some food.

'Have you eaten anything?' I asked Kasim.

'Yes, I have,' he replied shortly.

'What did you eat?' I knew that the last time he had eaten was the day before, in the morning.

'I had some scrambled eggs,' he said. I could see his mind was far away from this room. I decided not to ask many questions. While I was eating, he told me it was not safe to stay at home. He was sure that the Chetniks were coming back, if not to attack the village again then to take him away somewhere.

'What do you think we should do?' I wanted to know his opinion about the whole situation.

'You stay at home and I'll spend the night in the woods. If the Chetniks come to look for me tell them I went to Kozarac.' He put on some warm clothes, took his sleeping bag and rucksack, and left for the woods above our house.

I tended the animals and went back inside the house. I put the TV on to watch the news. I saw the interview conducted in the afternoon with Sero Velic, in which he was made to praise the army for treating us so kindly. Following this, I saw the TV Belgrade station claiming that: 'A few hundred Green Berets were captured in the Muslim village of Kevljani in north-western Bosnia, together with one thousand guns.'[6]

I switched the TV off. Would they let us stay in our homes after such news? I was frightened. All my thoughts were jumbled. I could not sort them out. I was tired but I had no time to rest. I was afraid of staying at home alone.

I shaved and washed my face. I was just brushing my teeth when I heard someone calling from the woods where Kasim had gone to hide.

'Green Berets, surrender.' This was followed by a couple of rifle shots.

'Here they are. Faster than I expected them,' I said to myself. I quickly took a small bag with some essentials that I had packed earlier, and went out of the house. Absurd to think of it now — but I had been brushing my teeth when I heard these chilling voices. As I walked down the road leading away from our house, I continued brushing my teeth out of some strange sense that this very ordinary activity would ground me while my reality was collapsing all around. I saw Kasim coming from the village centre. In the woods he had seen the Chetniks and so he had returned. He said this time they were brave enough to enter Kevljani, now they knew that nobody in the village was armed. Emir was behind him, carrying his packed bag. Both looked like refugees in their own village. Other people started coming out of their houses, too. Suddenly, none of us felt safe to stay indoors on our own. By now

---

6. Serbian propaganda fabricated a lie that the Bosnian government had an armed force ready to carry out genocide against their people. They named this 'force' 'Green Berets'.

it was certain that the Chetniks were coming back, but what exactly they intended to do nobody could tell. We expected the worst.

Standing on the road, we were joined by Zaim, Dido, Sedin and Asim. We tried to agree where to spend the approaching night. Nowhere seemed safe enough. We agreed that staying outdoors was riskier than going indoors. Dido went back into his house. 'If they're brave enough to come into my house during the night, they'll find me waiting behind the door with an axe,' he said.

Asim followed. Zaim, his two brothers and their parents decided to stay in the open, believing they were more likely to avoid any direct contact with the Chetniks. Kasim, Sedin and I went to Dido's house. Emir went to Serif's house, where many other villagers had been gathering.

The safest place in Dido's house was the hall, which was well protected by strong walls on all four sides. We turned out all the lights. Small groups of villagers on the road were still moving towards Serif's house. In case Kasim and I would not be able to return home in the morning, I wanted to take some more things with me now — so I ran back to our house. Reaching the cattle-shed, I spotted in the dark a small, white kid standing with its front legs on the doorstep. The Chetniks were already inside the village. I turned around and ran back to Dido's house.

'What happened? Why didn't you bring the things?'

'The door of the shed was open. I'm sure I closed it earlier.'

A group of people staying in Fuad's house had a clear view of our front yard. Armin, who spent the night there, told me the following morning that he had seen the Chetniks running across our front yard.

All this time there was sporadic shooting. As the night fell, the machine-gun fire became very intense. Tank and mortar fire followed soon after. From the bedroom, Dido brought out several blankets and pillows which we spread on the floor. Kasim wanted to stay close to the window overlooking the front yard. He lay beneath the kitchen table, and from time to time he had a look through the window. Around 10.00pm, somebody outside the house called Dido's name. It was Enes. We let him in. Twenty minutes later he told us his father, Fadil, was alone at home, and he asked Dido, 'Can I bring him to stay with us?'

'Of course you can.'

A bit later they came. The constant firing continued until 6.00am.

4

We tried to eat something. We heated up the bean soup that Dido had made earlier, but there was not enough bread for all of us.

'We have almost a whole loaf at home,' I said, 'I'll go home quickly and bring it here.'

The shed door was closed again. In the house, I quickly took our passports, my personal ID, a woollen blanket and two winter jackets. I also took the bread and went back to Dido's house.

We all agreed it was no longer possible to stay in the village. Dido suggested it would be a good idea to ring up some of his Serb mates from Radivojci, with whom he had played football for many years. He thought they might let us pass through their village in order to get to Kozarac. We did not know that the situation in Kozarac was no better.

Then a neighbour came and told us that the Chetniks had issued an order that the whole village must go back to the school once again. The incredible explanation for this move was that it was no longer safe for us to stay in the village. They were going to transport us by buses to Omarska. From there we were to go on to stay with our relatives in Prijedor or Banja Luka until the whole situation calmed down.

Minutes after this, another shock swept through the village. Redzep Hodzic had hanged himself. With his family and some neighbours, he had spent the previous night in Sero Velic's summer kitchen. When the firing stopped, he quietly got up and said: 'I'm going to check the cattle.'

There was nothing unusual about his behaviour, but his long absence made his sons anxious. They went home and found their father hanging on a tree in the garden. During the Second World War, Redzep had survived a long period of captivity. There was not enough time for a proper burial. They took his body off the tree and buried him in the garden.

Knowing what had happened to other towns and villages in Eastern Bosnia, we sensed that we were leaving the village for the last time. We released the animals so they would not suffer from starvation and thirst. This was the beginning of ethnic cleansing in Prijedor. Hundreds of years of our presence on this land vanished in the blink of an eye.

On the way to the school, Armin wanted to throw his army ID into a ditch beside the road. 'I don't need this any more,' he said.

'Keep it,' Kasim and I advised him. 'You never know, you may need it.'

Armin had just completed an extended period of National Service, which involved fighting against the Croats in the Zadar area. He was forced into it, but now such a record might be useful in saving his life. He kept the card. When we reached the school, we once more saw our Serb neighbours. Dusan 'Dudo' Loncar, Ranko Radivojac, Strahinja 'Prpo' Lukic, Aleksandar 'Aco' Zec were there — all holding rifles. I had known them all my life, and had been at school with Ranko and Prpo. From a distance, they kept an eye on us while we waited for the first buses to arrive.

When the first bus came, those who had survived the attack in Gornji Jakupovici two days earlier were placed in the front seats. Next to the driver sat a man in his fifties, a member of the Serbian Democratic Party (SDS) from Omarska, who had worked for years as a clerk at the local branch of Privredna Banka Sarajevo (PBS). His task was to organise our transport. The bus was quickly filled with the old, the sick, women and children.

While waiting to get on one of these buses, I became very thirsty. Opposite the looted village shop with broken windows and smashed doors there was a water well belonging to a Serb by the name of Lazo. I crossed the road and asked his mother Marija: 'May I have some water from your well?' She was doing some work around the house and paying no attention to the scene across the road.

'Sure,' she said. And she carried on with her work.

Time was passing slowly. The last two buses arrived at about 8.00pm. Kasim and I boarded the second one. It was impossible for all of us to fit into two buses. Those still waiting on the road were loaded onto two small pick-up trucks and two passenger cars. We started moving.

In Gornji Jakupovici, there was destruction all around. Houses had been hit by tank fire. Some had burnt to the ground; others were still burning. The shelling had stopped here two days earlier. The burning houses had been set on fire by neighbouring Serbs. All that was left of once beautiful homes were piles of rubble and ash. The owners, who had invested many years of hard work in the building of these houses, lost them in a matter of minutes. It was clear to us that our houses would end up this way, too. I said goodbye to my village. The pictures of horror in Gornji Jakupovici remained deeply carved in my mind.

We were heading towards Omarska. We passed through

evacuated Serb villages — the Chetniks having used this territory as a base for launching attacks on us. In Omarska, three Muslim women from Kamicani boarded the bus. Their village was far away and their presence here was puzzling. There were no signs of civilian life in Omarska. In front of every public building stood a couple of middle-aged armed men, dressed half in army, half in civilian clothing. The only passing civilian was Boja Delic, a Serb woman who grew up in the northern part of my village. Her eyes filled with tears when she saw us. A young soldier boarded the bus. He was our escort. The column moved on.

No one told us where we were being taken. One thing was clear — we were not going to spend ten days with our relatives either in Prijedor or in Banja Luka. We went through Omarska, crossed the flyover, passed the entrance gate of the mining complex, and headed towards nowhere. The journey lasted hours. I was not burning with desire to know what was waiting for us at the journey's end. I was sure it couldn't be anything good. We reached Cela, a Muslim village which had surrendered without resistance. Five or six drunk and disorderly Chetniks controlling the road block there stopped the column and insisted that we should all be shot. Others made an effort to calm them down. Talking briefly with our escort, they let us pass on towards Prijedor.

It was already after 10.00pm when we entered Prijedor. The town looked ghostly. Street lights were turned off and the windows of houses darkened. The curfew was on and the streets were deserted. The column stopped on the plaza in front of the Mladost sports centre.

In my student days at the Electrotechnical School, just behind the sports centre, the centre and the plaza were the main gathering places for students. In the evenings, and during weekends, the centre staged concerts — pop, rock, and Yugoslav folk music. In those days it was certainly the liveliest place in town. Now, it was once again filled with people. Women, children and the elderly who had arrived before us were being detained here.

On the plaza, there was a group of soldiers. Bus drivers and escorts left to join them, leaving the bus engines running. Opening the windows was strictly forbidden. We were all exhausted and parched. Twenty to thirty minutes later, our driver came back and opened the back door. Everybody on the bus wanted to get closer to it in order to get some fresh air. I was no more than two metres away from the door, but those next to it created another kind of barrier. They stuck their heads out and made it virtually impossible for any air to reach us inside the bus.

During this time, the soldiers on the plaza were discussing something. They obviously could not decide what to do with us. Finally, men were ordered to disembark from all the vehicles. Women and children had to stay inside. With hands up we left the vehicles one by one. A Chetnik was searching everybody — looking for any weapons.

'What's this?' He touched the roll of money in my back pocket.

'It's money.' I took it out and showed it to him.

'What's wrong with your voice? Why are you scared?'

'I'm not scared. I have a sore throat,' I lied. I was so exhausted, not only by this journey, but by everything that had taken place during the last six days, that I could hardly speak at all. As the search ended, we were put onto yet another bus. It was much smaller, with some twenty seats. About forty of us were forced aboard. The new escort, holding a Kalashnikov, pointed at us and shouted: 'You Turkish motherfuckers, one wrong move and I'll kill you all!'

He continued swearing and threatening and the bus driver joined in the abuse. 'We should slit your throats. You deserve nothing better,' the driver was snarling.

By braking suddenly, he would make us all lurch forward,

falling on those in front of us. Then he would start again abruptly and we would fall on those behind.

Eventually, we stopped at Keraterm, the ceramic tile factory. In peacetime, Keraterm was a symbol of success for the local economy. In these times, it would become a symbol of brutality.

Keraterm was already crammed with people. Several full buses queued in front of our vehicle. More men stood on the tarmac. Around 11.00pm, more buses arrived and these men were loaded on to them. There was now a long column of buses moving towards Bosanski Novi, a small town west of Prijedor. Then we turned off the highway and entered a small village, Brezicani. After many sharp turns on narrow roads, the column finally stopped in the front yard of the village primary school. The school yard was full of 'White Eagles' — irregular mercenary units recruited mainly from Serbia. They had dark blue berets with an insignia featuring a double-headed white eagle.

'Take your belongings and get off the bus.' The order was short and clear.

Leaving the bus with our hands raised, we received a shower of rifle butts over the head, the rib cage, and the spine, and were kicked with heavy boots in the stomach. Inside the school's corridor, the irregulars were grabbing people at random and beating the hell out of them. Inside the sports hall we were lined up, heads down and hands clasped behind the head. We remained in this position for some time. The White Eagles left, leaving the domestic Chetniks in charge. They ordered us to sit on the floor. The atmosphere was very tense. We did not know what to expect next. We were transported around like sacks of potatoes from one warehouse to another. I was in the grip of cold anxiety. I thought of Mama: 'Where is she now? Is she all right?' I wanted to believe that she at least was all right.

A group of women and children was brought in. The floor was cold, and we gave our blankets to the children to sit on.

The night never seemed to end. We were given neither food nor water. After repeated appeals, a plastic canister of water appeared. It contained traces of oil, but any water was better than no water at all.

'Why did you turn against us?' a bearded Chetnik in his thirties wanted to know. 'Why didn't you join us in the fight against the *Ustashe* in Croatia? Why did you plan to slaughter our children? We can kill you right here and now and no one would be any wiser. We can say you attacked us trying to escape.' We were numbed. Nobody replied.

Ilijaz Djihic, a middle-aged man from Kamicani, was sitting close to me. 'Guys,' he whispered, 'they're going to kill us all. Let's do something. There are so many of us. We can deal with them.' The idea was preposterous. The guards had guns and they would not hesitate to shoot. Djihic was probably getting panicky because he was wearing army trousers, shirt, jumper and shoes. He probably thought that if they wanted to kill someone, his clothes would seal his fate.

'Sit down and keep quiet,' we said, trying to calm him down, 'they'll kill no one.' He stopped talking, but his eyes stayed firmly fixed on the guards.

I asked myself: 'Where does this hatred come from?' I remembered my conversations with Mama earlier that year. A couple of times when Kasim was away from home, I had talked with Mama about war. She always feared for the safety of Kasim and me. I said to her that every type of war brings death. So it might happen that we, her sons, could become victims if a war came from Croatia. A very cruel way to talk to your mother. But only now could I realise how shallow my talk of war had been. Mama had survived the horrors of the Second World War. My grandfather's death had forced Mama and her five brothers and sisters — with the oldest only twelve years old — to live the rest of their lives without knowing fatherly love. Her father, Serif, had been killed after false charges had been brought against him. His Serb neighbours had accused him of terrorising their community during the war. However unjust his death had been, Mama never taught my brothers or me to hate Serbs because of this history. After all the suffering Mama had had to bear during the course of that war, and what followed in the years afterwards, the only thing that could be worse for her would be to lose one or two of her three sons. That would be too much for any human being — not only for Mama. Yet she accepted the fact that in a war like this one, we could die, too.

During the night, I talked to men from Kozarac, Gornji Jakupovici, and Kamicani. I tried to get a clearer picture of the events of the past three days.

Kozarac had made an attempt at defence. There was no adequate shelter that could have offered the town protection from shells and mortars. Many had fled to the woods in the hills. But these very woods were also shelled. People were killed, and it soon became clear that the number of casualties was going to be enormous unless something was done quickly. The safe surrender of women, children, and all those not willing to fight was negotiated.

They were to assemble at two designated points — one below the highway near a filling station, and the other in the hamlet of Susici. As one of these groups was passing along Marshall Tito Street towards the filling station, they were suddenly confronted by a tank. The crowd was huge, but very compact. The tank fired point blank into the middle of the crowd without warning. Heads, limbs, and other parts of bodies flew all over the place. The Chetnik who fired came out of the tank weeping and apologising, claiming: 'I didn't know these were women, children, and unarmed men. I thought they were fighters.'

At the petrol station, many of the men were taken inside a

building behind the station and slaughtered there. The butchers had rolled their shirt sleeves above the elbows, and their arms and long knives were covered in blood.

As the second group going to surrender in Susici approached the highway, they were met by the Chetniks, who split them into two groups: women and children on one side, and men on the other side. Standing among the men, Enes Erdic, a young man from Kozarac, recognised several local Chetniks — including Goran Borovnica, Dusko 'Dule' Tadic, and 'Tepo' from Vidovici. They were randomly selecting men and sending them to a nearby house. Another group of twenty to thirty men was herded inside the garage next to the house. Through a small opening, the Chetniks threw hand grenades into the garage. The noise of the explosions and the screams of the victims filled the air. Of the group taken inside the house, only one man came out again. He was recognised by a Chetnik friend who decided to spare his life. Inside the house he had seen a bathtub filled with the heads of those taken in there before him.

The people in Gornji Jakupovici had been attacked at around 2.00pm. The attack came from the direction of the Serb village called Janjici. A tank and two APCs were in front, and the infantry was scattered behind the vehicles and on both sides of the highway. The defenders of Jakupovici placed a tractor trailer loaded with timber as a barricade on the highway. The tank shattered the barricade. Fire from the anti-aircraft guns killed Hazim, one of these ill-equipped defenders, instantly. Two others, Fudo and Beco, were blown up by a mortar shell that landed directly in their trench. In the first couple of minutes, several more defenders died. The defence collapsed completely, and the tank continued firing at the surrounding houses.

There were also two Chetnik casualties. One of the defenders was hidden in the tall grass, and two Chetniks coming his way were unable to see him. When they came too close, the frightened defender leapt up and took the Chetniks by surprise. Several defenders had managed to withdraw towards Kozarac, while the rest had been captured.

These conversations went on until morning. The Chetniks had still not decided what to do with us. A guard came in and announced: 'One of you has a pistol in here.' A pistol? After all the searches we had been through, it would have been a miracle if someone had managed to smuggle in a needle.

'If that person gives us the pistol nothing will happen to him,' he continued.

We denied there was any pistol. Nobody had a pistol. We denied it again. He insisted. This went on for an hour. Finally, one of the guards ordered us to give up all sharp objects, such as razor blades, pens, pencils, even nail clippers, and to place them on the table where the other guards were sitting.

'What's this?' One of them waved a pack of razor blades. 'You planned to slit our throats!' Slit the throats of heavily armed guards with razor blades? By now I was sick and tired of insane accusations. Could they not at least invent some more sophisticated plots?

Women and children were then sent on to the Trnopolje camp. The day dragged on. Some men ventured to ask the guards what they intended to do with us. They said, 'We know as much as you do. We're waiting for further orders.'

At 10.00pm, we again boarded the buses — once more running through a crowd of Chetniks beating us. The experience of being moved around by night was frightening. The first thought that entered my mind was: 'They want to get rid of us in the dark — when there are no witnesses.' The next thought calmed me down a bit: 'If they wanted to kill us, they wouldn't bother moving us from place to place — they would surely save themselves all this hassle.' However, they seemed to make all their decisions on the spur of the moment.

We left for Prijedor. At the next stop, we were back at Keraterm. Some fifteen buses full of men from Kamicani and Kozarac waited there. The Chetniks standing around the buses shook their fists at us — swearing, although we could not hear their threats. The one that boarded our bus said: 'Don't try to attack me or I'll fire.' He said he wanted to know what had really happened in the Kozarac region in the last couple of days, but I was not convinced of his ignorance. He was a Muslim; his wife was a Serb. He had spent the last eight months fighting in Croatia. He said he had seen many atrocities.

We continued back along the route we had travelled the day before. 'They're taking us to the Manjaca camp,' somebody guessed.

We reached Omarska. The first buses stopped before the gates of the Omarska mining complex. I was petrified by the thought of the huge mining pits. They could accommodate thousands of bodies. The longer the buses stood before the gates, the more paranoid I became. Minutes turned into years.

The gates opened and the first buses passed through. Fear was growing all the time. I was choking. It was pitch dark. Disconnected thoughts flashed through my mind with the speed of lightning. 'Why should they bring us here in the middle of nowhere, in the middle of the night, if not to throw our bodies into the pits?' I thought.

The column stopped. I saw several buildings around us — and plenty of White Eagles.

'Get off the bus! Hurry!'

Then it began — get out; ferocious blows; running up the stairs; to the left; more blows; inside a room; join the rows of those already standing there; head down; hands clasped behind the head. Surreptitiously, I tried to locate Kasim. I spotted him and Asim two rows in front of me. I crouched and sneaked between the two rows and joined Kasim. It was a great feeling just to be with him again.

The time was two o'clock in the morning. We were allowed to sit on the floor. The room was small and some five hundred of us were herded inside. There was just a tiled floor with four walls around us, nothing else. I spotted the guys from my village who had been taken away in the lorry from the football pitch. They all stood next to a wall.

Exhausted from squatting, Asim and I rested a bit by leaning against each other, back to back. There was no space to lie on the floor. I still had a blanket, but for the time being it could be of no use. I dozed off. Minutes later, my head slipped off his shoulder and I came to with a start. The room was buzzing with irritating whispers. I had nothing to say. I was just tired. All of a sudden the whispers were silenced. Shots were fired outside. Omarska's first victims. Two men from Kamicani had been shot dead.

Next to me, Kasim was wrapped up in his own thoughts. What was he thinking about? The days he spent working in this place while it was still a construction site? Events leading up to this moment? About the days ahead? I did not interrupt his thoughts. I was simply exhausted.

The night was very humid and hot. There was no air to breathe. The only two small windows were closed. Nobody was allowed to go to the toilet during the night. We were given two small plastic canisters of water. Seven-and-a-half litres of water for five hundred men. We waited.

Part Two

———

Omarska

5

The door opened at 07.00am.

'You can go out to the toilet now. Don't push around the door,' a guard said.

The White Eagles were not around any more. We formed queues to use the two toilets available. Two men were allowed to go at a time, which made the whole process very slow. About a thousand people on our floor were supposed to use this facility. It was a real miracle that almost fifty men from my room managed to use it that morning. The rest of us had no choice but to wait for the next opportunity.

Throughout the entire period of my detention in Omarska, the toilets were available for our use for only thirty minutes in the mornings, and thirty minutes in the evenings, which were the times when the guards were changing shifts. Each of us could therefore use the toilet only once every thirty-six or even forty-eight hours. Later on, forty to fifty of us at a time would be taken outside the building to the grass near the 'Red House'.

The door closed. We waited. But we didn't know what we were waiting for. I kept quiet. Silent questions in my mind. Why are we here? Why doesn't anybody talk to us? What's going to happen next? We are not getting any food — so what does the denial of food mean?

Around 10.00 am another guard came to the door. He called out the names of Ilijaz Hadzic, Nijaz Sivac, Muhamed Velic, Mesud Foric, and Zijad Klipic.

One by one they left the room. The door closed. Silence. No one knew where they were taken. Medo Hadzic, the brother of Ilijaz, broke the silence. He had been held with these men at the police station in Omarska village before they were brought to the camp. At the police station, he had been the only one not afraid to talk to the policemen.

'You attacked unarmed civilians,' he told them. 'We are ordinary people, not soldiers. Couldn't you let us stay in our homes? We had no power to resist your army and you know that.' The policemen made no reply.

Why did Medo tell us this? Was it sheer frustration with this whole situation where we could do nothing but ask ourselves questions without finding any answers? Maybe he just needed to say something after his brother was gone. Maybe he felt he was not going to see him again.

The day was extremely hot. The heat of five hundred bodies, and the closed door and closed windows raised the temperature inside the room several degrees above that on the outside. Physical exhaustion, thirst, hunger, sweating, and constant tension nailed me to the floor. My body, used to consuming several regular meals a day, was finding it difficult to adapt to hunger. I was too weak to think. I squatted with my eyes closed. People talked. The whole room talked. The irritating salvo of their voices was painful to my eardrums. The constant buzz in the room was nerve-racking. I had never been a person who liked crowds. Living with this crowd for a couple of days had taken away all my privacy. I was thinking, 'I can't stand this any more. I'll go mad.' I felt an urge to stand up and shout, 'Shut up! All of you! No more fucking talking!' But I kept silent.

At 7.00pm, the door opened again. A new shift of guards had arrived. Time to use the toilet. The door remained open for about fifteen minutes. I didn't even try to get up and queue. I decided to wait until the following morning. Some people asked the guard at the door — we knew him, his name was 'Cvitonja' Pavlic — what they intended to do with us. He didn't know. They asked him if we were going to get some food. He knew, he said, as much as we did. We waited. The guards waited. None of us knew what we were waiting for. Uncertainty made the whole situation even more unbearable.

We were hungry. Asim 'Ako' Jakupovic, one of those who talked to Pavlic, asked if he would bring us some food for money. He said he would. We collected some two thousand German marks and Pavlic took the money, saying he couldn't possibly bring enough food for five hundred men. He closed the door.

The following morning, the door opened again at 7.00am. This time I was determined to use the toilet. Soon after I returned to the room, Pavlic brought a sack with some twenty loaves of bread, some milk croissants, and three bottles of milk. Kasim and I were amongst the lucky ones. About fifty grams of bread reached our hands.

Later in the day, another familiar face appeared in the corridor. It was Drasko Gruban, who used to work as a shop assistant in my village. He was a camp guard now. Asim Hodza spotted him and rushed to the door. They greeted each other and Asim asked if Drasko could bring us some cigarettes. Drasko promised he would bring two boxes of 'Herzegovina' cigarettes the next day. We were desperate for cigarettes. The next day Asim realised that Drasko had added his own personal commission to the price. Nevertheless, we bought them. The three of us, Kasim, Asim and I, kept three packs. We distributed the rest to other smokers around us.

We didn't know what was happening outside. We didn't know what the Serbs were planning to do with us, but at least we knew nobody was being killed. I started to talk. Kasim, Asim and I went through what had happened during the last couple of days and we concluded that — if we were released — we couldn't stay in the area any more. Even if we were allowed to return to our village, we decided that it would be too risky to remain there surrounded by the neighbouring armed Serbian villages.

'When we are free you'll go with me to Gradacac,' Asim said to Kasim and me. Gradacac was his birthplace. 'My father has plenty of land. He can afford to provide two housing allotments for the two of you.'

We were hungry. We talked about food. Asim was saying, 'We'll go to Gradacac and we'll cook *pekmez* [traditional Bosnian plum jam].' We passed the time with such conversations, but still the time dragged very slowly.

The second morning was identical to the first. Thirty minutes for the toilet, no food, another hot day inside the closed room. Later in the day, some vehicles arrived at the camp. They stopped on the tarmac area between our building and the administration building. The engines stayed running.

'It's buses,' somebody said cheerfully. 'They're going to release us. We're going home.' This joy was short-lived. The vehicles were indeed buses, but not for our release. More people seemed to have been brought in, we realised, as we could hear singing:

> *Who is it telling lies that*
> *Serbia is small?*
> *She is not small, she is not small.*
> *Three times she fought in a war,*

She'll fight again, and again,
She won't be a slave.
She'll fight again, and again,
She won't be a slave ...

The singing, accompanied by the noise of bus engines, lasted some two hours.

Later on, we learned that two buses with more than two hundred new inmates had been brought to the camp. They were men who had refused to surrender, and for the past few days they had been hiding in the woods of the Kozara Mountains. Eventually, they were captured by Serbian soldiers and the local militia. When they disembarked from the buses, the 'White House' received its first tenants. A small number of those that the 'White House' could not accommodate were locked in the small garage behind the administration building.

Their arrival shattered every dream of a possible early release.

We were given no food for the first four days. Then Ljuban Anjdic, son of one of the local 'heavies', entered our room and made a short announcement.

'I'm here to provide you with medical care and to organise the work of the canteen. You will receive one meal per day.'

Ljuban left and a guard at the door issued the order: 'Fall into groups of fifteen.' Good news. We were going to eat. On the other hand, it was bad news. It was a confirmation that they had no intention of releasing us. Everybody wanted to get to the canteen first. But Asim, Kasim and I didn't hurry. I had neither the will, nor the energy to push to the front. The first group left the room. Five minutes later they returned — running and puffing. The guards considered walking a waste of time. The next group left the room.

There were thousands of us in the camp. It was going to take the whole day for everyone to pass through the canteen. When it was our turn, we left the room running — through the corridor, down the stairs, and across a short distance between the two buildings where we entered the canteen. Looking around was strictly forbidden. After four days of being cooped up within four walls, it was a relief to breathe some fresh air.

The canteen was in the administration building. There was a serving counter, and eight tables with four chairs each. I received a tiny slice of bread and a plate of 'soup' — greyish water with about ten peas in it. It was cold and sour. There was no need for spoons. I lifted the plate and poured it down my throat. I took the bread, put it in my pocket and left the canteen running again. Back in the room, I ate the bread — undisturbed by the presence of the Chetniks and their yelling.

'I had never eaten peas before in my life,' Kasim said to me back in the room.

'Was it good?' I teased him.

'From now on, I'll eat nothing but peas,' he said seriously. After so many days without food we were prepared to eat anything. Good or bad, food meant survival.

This system of food distribution had many pitfalls. The camp authorities had no clue who had been in the canteen and who had not. They never tried to make lists of our names. Some men saw this as an opportunity to sneak to the canteen twice. They would eat twice while others would get nothing. The guards threatened that anyone caught trying to eat twice would be beaten severely. But they never bothered to memorise faces that had already passed through the canteen once. A few days after the canteen became operational, we ourselves made a list of names of everyone in Room 24, which put an end to thieving. Some inmates, though, risked quickly pouring two plates of soup into one. Still, the list helped guarantee all men their ration — as long as enough food had been delivered to allow everyone at least the usual meagre portion.

After one week the guards increased the number of people in

one group to thirty, as the canteen had a capacity to receive thirty-two men. Also, as the first group was running to the canteen, the next group was leaving the building, and waiting on the tarmac area. The three-minute limit for eating had the worst impact on the last men in every group. Just as they were collecting their soup, the Chetniks were already yelling: 'Haven't you finished yet? Faster, faster! Okay. Time's up. Get out now.' They had to drink up the soup in one gulp. Once I had to gulp down some soup that was almost boiling.

If and when the soup arrived, it was delivered to the camp on a small yellow lorry. On its return journey, this same lorry was loaded with the bodies of inmates murdered the night before.

6

The Omarska iron-ore mining complex was developed in the first half of the 1980s, and was a subsidiary of the biggest iron-ore mine in Europe. The Serbian attack on Slovenia and Croatia had brought production to a halt.

At the time of the Serbian assault on Bosnia, the mining complex lay idle. It was in the middle of the Chetnik heartland. Most of those who attacked Croatia had been recruited from the surrounding villages of Maricka, Jelicka, Gradina, Tomasica and Omarska.

The Omarska camp was set in a wide-open area. It was not fenced off. It was surrounded by rings of guard posts, and anyone attempting to escape would have been shot several times before reaching the far-off woods. There were four main buildings. The central building dominated the whole complex. At different points in time, it housed some two-thirds of the inmates. Facing this building, across a narrow tarmac area, was a small rectangular structure which became notorious as the 'White House'. On the left of the central building there was a small, isolated red brick building which we called the 'Red House'. And on the right of it, there was the administration building. The fifth incarceration facility was an open tarmac area lying between the administration building and the central building. It became known as the 'pista' (the 'runway').

The night we were brought to the camp, Kasim, Asim, and I ended up in Room 24 of the central building. The central building had two floors. On the ground floor, there was a big hall which must have been used as a garage for the repair of vehicles and machinery when the mine was in operation. On the far left end of the garage, there were two doors. One led to a tiny room without windows — and some forty to sixty men were squeezed in there. The staircase behind the second door led to a single room on the first floor. Some five hundred men were squeezed into this room, spilling over the staircase and the lockers under it. Another staircase led from the front entrance to the first floor, which contained seven rooms. At the top of the stairs, on the right, was Room 15. At the end of a long corridor, opposite Room 15, was Room 24. On the left side of the corridor, two smaller rooms occupied by the guards overlooked the 'White House'. Into each of the three small rooms opposite the guards' rooms, thirty to forty older men were crammed (the size of each room was approximately ten to twelve square metres). Some slept on the tables previously used as desks, while others slept on the floor. One of these smaller rooms was later converted into a 'living cemetery'. Those with no hope of survival for longer than a week spent their last moments there. Some were old men exhausted by lack of food and water, while others suffered from high blood pressure or diabetes. All were in need of constant medical care, but Omarska was not a place where they could hope to receive assistance.

Room 24 had formerly been used as a locker room. The lockers had been removed to pack inside as many of us as possible. There were two small windows on the wall facing the 'White House'. For several weeks we were not allowed to open them, even though the heat and the five hundred people crammed into the room created conditions similar to those of a tropical forest. It was not at all clear why we were not allowed to open the windows.

'You might attempt suicide by jumping from them,' a guard 'explained'.

The real reason was probably that we weren't supposed to see the torture and the killings that went on around the 'White House'. If so much as a shadow was seen near the window, the punishment was brutal. Yet some men couldn't resist the temptation. On one occasion, the guards rushed into the room and started beating all the people near the window. A man called Hasan got the worst of it. He had deep cuts on his head.

The morning after our arrival, the White Eagles were no longer there. The local Chetniks were now in charge of the camp. The first commander was a policeman from Omarska, Miroslav Kvocka. He always wore camouflage fatigues, expensive sun glasses, a dark blue beret and fingerless black leather gloves, and carried a Thompson gun. Several weeks later he was replaced by another policeman, Zeljko Meakic, from Petrov Gaj. During Kvocka's reign many inmates died, but under Meakic's control the camp would became a slaughterhouse.

Administrative control of the camp was in the hands of Dragoljub Prcac, a former employee of Prijedor's Ministry of Internal Affairs. The camp was guarded by three shifts. The shift leaders were Mladen 'Krkan' Radic, a policeman from Omarska; Momcilo 'Ckalja' Gruban, a former employee of the mine; and Milojica 'Krle' Kos, a waiter from Kosovi — a Serb hamlet near Omarska. They were all ruthless in their treatment of the inmates, but Radic surpassed the others in cruelty. He was not only a killer, but also an alleged rapist who had victimised several women inmates.

Every shift of guards was divided up into groups, with each group controlling a part of the camp. Two of the group leaders controlling the first floor of the central building, where I spent the entire period of my detention, were Rade Ritan, the salesman from Omarska, and Branko Pirvan from the Tomasica–Maricka area.

Some of the guards were unknown to me, but most were our neighbours, former schoolmates, classmates, even a deskmate. At first, they seemed ill at ease. There was some kind of hesitation and tension in their behaviour. They asked no questions and didn't talk too much. They were neither aggressive nor abusive.

I had known some of the guards personally. One of them was Milojica Beric, a neighbour from Berici, a group of houses set about a kilometre north of my house. He had been a classmate of mine for four years. In one of the first few weeks of our detention, I was running with twenty-nine other guys to the canteen. Milojica was sitting on a chair next to the entrance of the administration building. When I came close to him, he asked lazily: 'How's it going, Kemo?'

'It will be better,' I answered while running.

'It will be, it will be,' he repeated after me.

After this short, weird conversation, I never had verbal contact with Milojica again. When I saw him around, he never bothered to look at us.

There were two other guards who sometimes spoke to me — the Milutinovic brothers, Milan and Milorad. Before I was brought to the camp, I had known Milan for thirteen years. During my primary school days in Omarska, he had been my deskmate for a couple of years. Milorad was two years older than us, and he had attended the same school. Here, in the camp, Milorad was guarding inmates at the 'pista'. During the day, he would see me going to the canteen. As if it were some other place, somewhere where ordinary people go about their daily business, he would say: 'Hello, Kemo. How are you?' What could an inmate reply?

'Hi.'

I didn't want anyone to recognise me. All I wanted was to be invisible. I didn't want him to say anything to me — but when he did, I prayed our exchange would end with this brief greeting. I didn't want his fellow guards to notice me. I didn't want them to ask him, 'Who is the guy you just greeted?' I was not in a position to ignore them. I didn't want to discover what their reaction would be if I remained silent. Still, it was better to hear 'hello' than 'hey, you motherfucker'. Even when such encounters took place without the other guards present, I strictly avoided it. When Milan came across me in the corridor leading to Room 24, I wanted to turn away and go straight back to my room. I was unable to. My former schoolmate was standing here in front of me. He wore olive-green army trousers and a shirt with sleeves rolled up above his elbows. In one of his hands, he held a rifle. Such a bizarre situation.

'Hi Kemo,' he said.

'Hi.' Was this what the conflict was all about? Attack your neighbours. Kill your neighbours. And if somebody survived, you say to them: 'Hi. I know we had lived together, had attended the same schools together, had played football together, had had drinks together many a time, but you must understand — this is nothing personal. My loyalty to my people comes before humanity — before friendships.' Milan didn't have to say that. I knew that's what he meant.

'Is "Strucnjak" in here?' He was looking for my neighbour, Samir Pervanic — who had been given this nickname (meaning 'expert') by our biology teacher many years before.

'He's in that room over there.' I pointed over his shoulder to

Room 15. 'I have to go now. I'm not allowed to stay in the corridor.' I wanted him to go to hell. Before they attacked us, I had thought we had respect for each other. Ten days before the attack, I had talked to Milan — at the filling station in Omarska owned by his grandfather. He'd acted as if everything had been normal, while at home he had probably been keeping the same gun he now held in his hand.

Some weeks later (after changes in the camp regime which I will describe below), there were stories that every guard member was required to kill somebody in the camp. It was said that those refusing to participate in these orgies of violence would be forced by others to take an active part, so that later they could not say they had not been involved in killings. I remember times when Mile Rosic, the quietest guard inside the camp — who never shouted at an inmate — was told by the more extreme ones: 'Rosic, you have to do what we all do.'

'I don't want to,' he would respond. But days later, he was shouting at those he did not recognise (those of us from Kevljani would pass by him without being shouted at — for he knew us all). I could see that there was no passion and fire in it like that displayed by those genuine Chetniks — Chetniks by will and not Chetniks by force. I hope at least Mile was not amongst those who had covered their hands in the blood of the innocent.

Everything changed when a special police squad from Banja Luka arrived to teach these 'amateurs' how to run the camp. These 'specialists' created such an atmosphere of fear that nobody dared to use the toilet if even just one of them was seen in the corridor. We were hoping they would leave again soon, as their presence had made going for meals a risky business. The wait outside the building for the group before me to finish their meal sometimes seemed like an eternity. We were completely exposed to the guards walking around. Drasko Gruban, the guard who had brought us cigarettes, told Kasim to avoid attracting attention. 'Just keep out of their way and keep a very low profile.' This proved good advice, especially later on when accidental eye contact could cost lives. One silly move and the guards would pounce on you. In those early days there was a guard, no older than eighteen or nineteen, who had the look of a mad dog. He was very hostile towards every single inmate. He never spoke, but always shouted. In the evenings, when selected victims were subjected to ferocious beatings, I could always recognise the sound of his voice swearing at the victim.

Standing one morning in a queue for a meal, I saw 'Mad Dog' coming along the queue and asking each person the same question. When he came to me, he repeated it.

'Do you know Adem Blazevic?' He was asking about a man who had already been killed earlier in Kozarac, but he obviously didn't know that.

'No, I don't.'

'What's your name?'

'Kemal Pervanic.'

'Where are you from?'

'Kevljani.'

'Where is Kevljani?'

'Some five kilometres from here.'

'Have you got any family members or cousins in Bihac?'

'No, I haven't.'

'Do you know anybody there?' He probably wanted to know whether I had any connection with Bihac at all.

'No, I don't.'

I was very tense and ill at ease. He questioned me longer than the others. He seemed to have connected my surname with something or somebody. I had already learned that knowing somebody the guards had a grudge against was dangerous. In the absence of the one they were looking for, anyone related to him, or even those who just knew the man they were seeking, would do just as well. He continued down the queue asking about Blazevic.

Other Chetniks simply liked to come and stand in front of you and scrutinise you without a word. This weird practice gave me the creeps. 'Mad Dog' was looking for a particular person, but these guys were doing it for fun. Once a member of the special police squad from Banja Luka went down the queue scrutinising everybody in this way. My long hair always attracted attention. Lifting my hair with his truncheon he asked, 'What's this?'

'It's hair,' I replied with an equally stupid answer. The words just fell out of my mouth.

'Why do you have long hair?'

'I like to listen to hard rock and heavy metal.'

It was not the reason why I had long hair, but it was the first short answer that sprang to mind and that I could squeeze through my tightening throat. I was petrified.

'Which groups do you listen to?'

'Deep Purple, AC/DC ...'

'Led Zeppelin,' he interrupted me.

'Yes.' I was in luck. He seemed to like this music, too. He was apparently not a fan of cheap Serbian nationalistic songs.

I was petrified on account of Kasim, too. He was standing right behind me and had already been marked out by this Chetnik earlier on. Two days earlier, Sakib Pervanic had jumped the toilet queue. When Sakib was on his way back to the room, this same Chetnik slapped him.

'Do you think you're better than others?'

'No.' Sakib bowed his head.

'Why did you jump the queue then?' Sakib did not answer.

'Get back in there,' the Chetnik nodded towards the room.

The day after this incident, the same Chetnik came to our room, and spotting Sakib beckoned: 'You — the hairy one! Come out here.'

'Me?' Sakib asked in fear.

'Yes, yes you.'

Sakib left the room. Half an hour later he was back. The Chetnik then called Kasim out. Why Kasim? He did not know Kasim. I sat there hopelessly. I knew people were being killed. I feared for him because he had owned a weapon. Nobody around me asked any questions. Some just stared at me. I was quiet. I didn't know what to think. I waited nervously. When Kasim came back he was very quiet, as if he were bearing a heavy burden on his shoulders.

'Where were you? What happened?'

'I was in the guards' room,' he said.

When he entered the guards' room, two other guys, Rasim Hodzic from our village and Mujo Jukic from Garibi, were already in there. Both men were standing before a desk, keeping their heads down and their hands clasped behind their backs. On the desk there was a piece of paper with five names. The last two men were brought in after Kasim. They all had one thing in common. They had all possessed arms. The only logical conclusion was that Sakib had written their names down. The Chetnik asked questions about their arms. For every answer that did not satisfy him he used karate chops. Blood from Rasim's nose was dripping on the floor. Kasim received several kicks. They all returned to their rooms, but they were clearly marked out.

Now, standing in the meal queue, I feared this Chetnik would pick on Kasim again. But he did nothing. Nevertheless, on our way back to the room he stood at the entrance to the building. He raised his truncheon saying: 'You motherfucker, I've been waiting for you,' and he hit Kasim hard.

Kasim did not stop. He kept running. Back in the room, he took his shirt off and exposed two huge welts.

'A picture on a picture,' Sejo laughed.

It was quite late. Another hot summer day was coming to an end.

Today the yellow lorry arrived in the afternoon. Since early morning we had wondered if we would get any food at all. My room was the last one to go to the canteen, and my group was the last one for the day. Today the Chetniks did not seem to be in the mood for beating. They stood around waiting for the replacement shift to come. A young policeman from the Banja Luka squad stood smoking a cigarette. He was my height and had straight brown hair. He wore blue camouflage fatigues and civilian boots. His sleeves were rolled up to his elbows.

'Hey, you,' he said, looking at me. 'Will you step out of the queue for a moment?' I went towards him. 'Will you untie your hair and let it hang?' I pulled off the rubber band with which my hair was tied in a bun — as I hoped that in this way it would be less conspicuous.

Fear was choking me. What did he want from me? It was getting dark and the worst possible place to be when darkness fell was standing there on the 'pista'. Nobody ever went out to the 'pista' after dark, as that was the time when the killers were prowling about. My heart felt like it would jump out of my chest. I felt a desperate need to take a couple of very deep breaths. I needed more oxygen. I did my best to appear to be breathing easily, hoping that my anxiety was not too obvious.

'What's your name?' he asked, smiling.

'Kemal Pervanic.'

'Where are you from?'

'From Kevljani. It's a village some five to six kilometres from here.' I pointed towards Kozarac, which was behind my village.

'How do I know that you are who you claim to be?'

'I have my ID card here.' I pulled it out of my pocket and showed him the page with personal details. He nodded.

'Where were you during the war in Croatia?'

'At home.' I wondered why he wanted to know that.

'All the time?'

'That's right. All the time.'

'Weren't you by any chance with Zagorci at Pakrac last Autumn?' Zagorci were Croatian soldiers from the northern region of the country.

'No, I wasn't.'

'There's no need to lie to me. If you are the right person I can help you.'

'Why should I lie to you? You can easily find out who I am. I'm telling you the truth.'

'Last year at Pakrac, I was in a big group of refugees. A guy, who looked exactly like you, saved my life. The same long blond hair. The same blue eyes. He was your height, and his face was just like yours. He was with a group of Zagorci. He kept his M84 machine gun pointed at me. He could have killed me on the spot, but he smiled and gave me a nod to pass. If you are the same man I can help you.'

'No, I'm not that guy.'

'Are you sure?' he asked again with a rascal's smile.

'I'm sure,' I repeated, but didn't smile back. Feverish questions raced through my mind. 'What does he mean "*I can help you*"? Are we in some kind of danger that he knows about and we don't?'

'Do you smoke?' He offered me a cigarette. I accepted it. A short pause — then the question I dreaded most.

'Shall we go upstairs?' He gestured toward the administration building, where interrogations were held.

We strolled towards the building. Several young men from the same police unit were sitting on a blue APC.

'Hey, what's that? Is it a girl?' I kept walking. I was not quite sure whether I should ignore them or respond in some way. I hoped this guy would help me. He did. One of these guys said more loudly: 'Hey you! I'm talking to you!'

'Leave him alone,' the policeman said, 'he's with me.' They just laughed.

He came to the first floor and entered the first room on the left. I followed. The room was small. There was a desk in the middle with an office chair behind it and two chairs in front. He sat behind the desk and offered me one of the two chairs.

'How old are you?'

'Twenty-four.'

'Oh really? We're the same age then. I'm twenty-four myself. I am Pero Vragas,' he added, introducing himself for the first time. 'I lived in Pakrac before the war started. When the Croats forced us out, I came to Banja Luka and joined the special police unit. We had special training to be prepared to intervene at any time, anywhere in the region.'

He was very polite all the time, but I still didn't know what he wanted. By now, I began to relax a bit. My heart rate was normal again, and the choking feeling in my throat was gone. I still felt anxious though. I could not afford to relax too much. He put his cigarettes on the desk.

'Help yourself,' he said, offering me another cigarette. I took one and was about to put the pack back on the desk when he surprised me, saying: 'You can have it all. I have another whole pack.' He pulled it out of his shirt pocket. Lighting my cigarette, he asked once more whether I was the guy he persistently insisted I might be.

'Look,' I said, 'there is a man by the name of Svetozar Petrovic, he used to be my maths teacher. You can check with him everything I've told you so far. He knows me well.' I didn't mention that some of my former schoolmates were camp guards. They could always confirm my identity, but as the behaviour of the guards was always unpredictable I preferred to leave them out of it. Suddenly he changed the topic.

'What happened in your village? How did you end up in here?'

'We were shelled by artillery on 24 May. After a night in the local river bed we surrendered.'

'What's the name of your village again?'

'Kevljani.'

'What do you know about organising defence in your village?'

Finally — here we are. This was what he really wanted. This conversation had nothing to do with Zagorci and Pakrac. He wanted to carry out some private investigation. Maybe he was bored and had decided to test his interrogating skills.

'There was no defence in my village.'

'What do you know about guys who had guns?'

'I don't know that any guys had guns.'

'You know,' he said, 'if you help us find the guys who were involved in organising defence, and those who fought against us, we can help you a lot. We can give you a pass for the whole of Bosnian Krajina. You would be able to move everywhere freely. You can get out of here. Maybe even if I'm near your village, I could drop by your place for a cup of coffee.'

'I really don't know. If I did I'd tell you.'

The door opened and two guards came in. They both wore civilian police uniforms. The older and taller one was Zdravko Govedarica. I also knew the other one. We were both at the same primary school in Omarska. Hitting the palm of his left hand with his truncheon Govedarica asked Pero: 'Is he a good boy? If he isn't just tell us.'

'Yeah, he's all right,' Pero smiled. The second guard sat on the free chair, holding his Kalashnikov between his legs.

'Where are you from?' he asked me.

'Kevljani.'

He suddenly launched into how resistance was given to their army when Kozarac was attacked, and how some young Serbs died during the attack. I itched to ask how many of us had been killed during that same attack — how many women and children. But all I could say was: 'I really don't know what happened in Kozarac. We surrendered immediately. None of us fired back.'

I concentrated hard on avoiding making them angry in any way. I was racking my brain trying to guess the best way to save my skin. This was extremely tiring. I couldn't predict what their next reaction might be. It seemed to me that the best I could do was to stay as calm as possible, and hope they were not going to beat the hell out of me.

'I just came back from Vlasic. It's fucking difficult to be there, and in ten days I have to report back to my unit.' I made no comment.

Then the guards left. Closing the door behind them, Govedarica said to Pero once again: 'If he gives you any trouble just call us in. We'll be waiting outside.'

Pero asked me to switch on the light. I lit another cigarette. He still wanted me to give him some information, any information. The pressure was mounting.

'Just give me a couple of names. They don't have to be involved in anything I asked you about. Just give me several names.' The pressure became unbearable.

'How can I give you the names of people who did nothing wrong? I can't do that.'

'Nobody will ever know.'

I had lost any sense of what it was he hoped to achieve with this.

'I can't do that. Put yourself in my shoes.'

I could give him several names on a piece of paper. He was right. Nobody would know. But if I survived, it would haunt me forever. To give him names would be the same as killing those people myself.

'But you have to.' He was still smiling. He didn't say this angrily. He did not raise his voice.

I dropped my head. For a minute or two I said nothing. The room was charged with a palpable tension. I started shaking my head. He carried on: 'Okay. Let's do it this way. Don't write down any names. I'll come tomorrow to your room. When you see me just look at a person. Nobody will ever know.'

Ten, fifteen seconds later I managed to ask: 'May I go back now?'

'Okay,' he said. 'When we get there I'll push you through the door and act nasty so nobody will suspect.'

'All right.' I put the cigarettes he gave me in my pocket.

'I can't give you the lighter,' Pero said. 'This is the only one I have.'

It was very late. The sky was very clear, and the stars seemed to be within reach. Pero pushed me back inside my room, saying: 'And remember. Next time be more careful.' At that moment, five hundred pairs of eyes looked at me. Five hundred mouths were wide open. They had not expected me to come back. The door closed behind me.

'Where were you?' Kasim looked very distressed. The two hours I was away had obviously seemed like centuries to him. He didn't know why I had been taken. He did not know whether I would be back. I was totally exhausted. I was mentally drained. The other men squeezed in a bit, making some room for me so that I could lie down.

'Lie down and rest,' Mesud tapped my shoulder. I could not say a single word. When I relaxed a bit I told them what had happened. I also explained that Pero was coming back in a day or two, and I asked if when he came they could gather around me and hide me. Far away from the door, Pero would have no chance to spot me.

Two days later, Pero came to the door. He looked around briefly, and left. A few days later he left with the special police squad for Banja Luka. Obviously his interview with me was nothing more than a game to pass the time. If he'd wanted to, he could have found me. After all, he knew my name.

The local guards, who were at first hesitant in their behaviour towards us, soon proved to be eager pupils. The lambs that at first seemed embarrassed to face us suddenly turned into wild beasts — of which there were two distinct breeds. The first ones were those incapable of thinking and judging for themselves. They were like a pack of hunting dogs, waiting for their master to give the order 'kill!' — whereupon they would readily jump and crush the victim to death. The second breed were those who would only half-kill their victim — keeping him alive for the next day. For the first group, this was impossible. Once engaged in beating, the life of their prey could be numbered in minutes. But the victims of the guards of the second breed were destined to die more slowly. They suffered excruciating torture day after day, night after night. One of their first victims was Azur Jakupovic. His story became a symbol of all such torments.

Azur Jakupovic was from Redak — a small village some two kilometres north from the part of the highway where the first attack started. For many years, he had lived in Banja Luka. He was a typical adventurer. But some two years before the attack, he had returned to his native village and opened a café, which soon became a popular gathering place. When it became apparent that the attack was imminent, Azur and a group of his mates armed themselves.

Once the fighting broke out, it became clear that Kozarac could not be defended. The only option the people had was unconditional surrender. Azur and his group then headed across the Kozara Mountain. They hoped to cross the Sava River into Croatia. During this period, several groups like Azur's were hiding in the woods of the Kozara Mountain. At the same time, the woods were flooded with the Chetniks who were trying to catch them. If given any resistance, the Chetniks executed them on the spot. It was best to travel during the night. This is where Azur and his group made a mistake. They rested at night and travelled during the day. Once they reached the plains of Bosnian Posavina, they became clearly visible for kilometres around. The Chetniks had men who constantly observed all the movements in this area. It did not take them long to spot Azur's group. Challenged to surrender, they ran. One was killed and Azur got shot in the leg. They were brought to Omarska.

Azur was tortured day after day and night after night. Each time, the Chetniks made sure that some life remained in him for the following day. Inexplicably, in spite of torture and non-existent hygiene conditions, his leg was getting better. The Chetniks inserted rusty wire into his wound. His screams reverberated throughout the camp. He sounded like a trapped, wounded animal that could not die. On the way to the canteen, I could see him sitting on the grass in front of the 'White House' under the watchful eyes of the guards, wiping the blood off his body.

Despite his wounded leg, he was forced to walk from the 'White House' to one of the offices on the first floor of the administration building. I once saw him walking across the 'pista', as if in slow motion, with an expression of great pain on his face.

One day a former army officer who had a grudge against Azur came from Banja Luka. He had come to settle his debt, but when he saw Azur he took pity on him. Even he was shocked by the cruelty of the camp guards who had turned him into a living corpse. By this time, Azur had attended several interrogations — each time admitting all the charges brought against him.

After the last interrogation, he could no longer leave the building without assistance. What the Chetniks carried out in a blanket was not Azur any more. He was alive — but he had only one eye. That eye was still shining with defiance against those who were seeking to annihilate us simply for who we were. He still found enough strength to spit at them. Then the clock stopped ticking for Azur Jakupovic — the man who never managed to harm a single Chetnik. He was not a hero — just an ordinary bloke who wanted to defend his homeland against those who had invaded it from within and without. But Omarska made a martyr of him.

Murder of men like Azur showed that the local camp guards had successfully completed the training given by the special police squad from Banja Luka. They had tasted blood. Killing did not mean taking the life of another human being any more. It had become a habit — their daily routine. Their teachers must have been proud of them.

Nobody was spared on the way to the canteen and back. Sometimes the guards would just shout at us to run and eat faster. But most of the time they kicked us and beat us with truncheons, whips, cables, and pipes. They played games. They would spill water on the tiled floor of the corridor leading to the canteen. Coming round the corner we could not see it. If one of us slipped, several of us would fall on top of him. Then they would gather round the heap of fallen men. A torrent of kicks, punches, and rifle butts hailed down on them. One of the early victims was Sejo. He returned to the room puffing — showing his welts and bruises and asking how bad it looked. Kasim said to me: 'A picture on a picture.'

Another game involved a bench at the entrance of the building in which the canteen was located. Running to the canteen, we had to jump over it. When the guards realised that most of us could hurdle it fairly easily, a guard always stood at each end of the bench. They would lift it unexpectedly, tripping the hurdlers. As we were certain to miss out on the Barcelona Olympics, I guess they thought they should organise local summer games. Some of those who tripped on the way back from the canteen would drop their piece of bread.

'Whose bread is this? Come back and pick it up,' the guards yelled. Nobody ever went back.

On special occasions, not only did *everybody* receive a meal, but we got a special 'treat' too. When an army helicopter landed bringing a group of high Serbian military officials to the camp, the guards showed off their skills by making sure that every single inmate got a blow from a truncheon — on his back when entering the canteen, and on his head when leaving it. As usual, Kasim and I let a few groups go before us. When the first group came back to the room, they were all panting. Nobody had had time to eat bread in the canteen, and no-one was spared from back-breaking and mind-blowing truncheons. I said to Kasim: 'I don't feel like having a dessert today.'

'Neither do I,' Kasim replied.

'Let's fast for another twenty-four hours. It's not the habit of "Turks" to hurry.' We remained in the room.

Time for eating was further restricted when the camp population increased to the maximum. Each group then had only ninety seconds. After leaving the canteen, we did not go straight back to our room. We had to assemble on the grass in front of the 'White House'. We sat there as live targets, the guards aiming at us with their rifles from the window of the guards' room. Sitting there helplessly made me realise the power of the rifle. From my place, the gun barrel staring at me seemed big enough for my head to fit inside it. That piece of steel could issue a bullet — a tiny piece of metal with the power to crush my skull and blow my brains out in a fraction of a second. It had the power to stop my life, which had been evolving for almost a quarter of a century. I wondered — if I had been at the other end, holding that rifle and aiming at the guard — would he have had the same thoughts? My thoughts were interrupted by his shots hitting the rubbish bins placed around us. When this happened, the guards standing nearby would laugh: 'Oh boy, that was close.'

On the way back to our room, a stolid oaf of a guard by the name of Stevan Tevanovic stood guard at the building entrance. He hit everyone indiscriminately. I would try to sneak by the wall hiding behind others. His bovine shape and strength would deliver blows with such force that once a guy from my room was thrown against a glass door, shattering the glass. The guy picked himself up and escaped upstairs.

'Who broke the glass? Come back!' Stevan yelled. The 'culprit' didn't even consider returning.

'If he doesn't come out I'll pick ten others and break their backs!' Eventually, we negotiated a damage settlement. The guards accepted the deal.

Among the early victims was a group of men from Garibi. When the Serb army attacked the Kozarac region, the small village of Garibi resisted. A bunch of villagers armed with Kalashnikovs fired at the approaching army. They refused to surrender until their resistance was crushed. Amongst the survivors were all six Garibovic brothers and their three neighbours, Ferid Garibovic, and the Jukic brothers, Mujo and Hamed. There was a special reason for them to come first on the waiting list. Zeljko Meakic had been their neighbour, and he was the man who ran the show in the camp. During the guards' 'training period', he kept the men from Garibi in anxiety. They were not ill-treated, but they knew it wouldn't stay that way for long. They knew he was preparing something for them.

Eventually, four of the six brothers and their neighbour Ferid were taken out at night. We heard screams and the sounds of beatings. After a while, the screaming stopped. Some of those from the 'pista' saw the guards throw the men's broken bodies on to the tractor trailer. They were still alive. The tractor moved behind the camp buildings. Minutes later continuous gunfire was heard in the distance. Their lives had been extinguished forever.

During one of the evenings following their deaths, Djemal, the oldest of the Garibovic brothers, ended up inside the central building. It was raining and the guards herded everyone from the 'pista' inside the buildings. Djemal saw Kasim inside our room, and he came to talk to him. His other living brother, Hilmija, was in the small room in the garage together with some guys from our village. Djemal told us what had happened in Garibi village and about his sense of foreboding. He knew that he and Hilmija could not be safe with Zeljko around. They were not. Soon after, they were executed, too. Mother Garibovic had lost all six of her sons.

The Jukic brothers ended up very much the same way. Hamed was killed early on in the camp. Mujo faced a more brutal death. Rumours spread that he had been taken to the police station in Omarska village where he was hanged. What he had had to endure before his death remains a secret.

After this group exercise, there was nothing else the guards could learn. They became professionals. Beating and killing was now their job. They rested only during their lunch hour and during coffee breaks. From then on the 'White House' became like a sinister bus station. Many people passed through it, but for most of them it was the last stop of their lives.

Sometimes the guards killed to celebrate. June 28 was St Vitus's Day — the anniversary of the Battle of Kosovo, where Serbia had lost to the invading Turks back in 1389. For many Serbs, it is the most sacred day in their lives. On June 28 1992, when the guards came on duty, they were spruced up, clean-shaven, and wearing smart civilian clothes. A fire was lit in front of the 'White House'. They roasted a pig — a traditional meal on this day — and ritually carved it with a dagger. They garnished it with the customary corn bread and plenty of home-made plum brandy. The radio played music which ominously suggested it was going to be an unforgettable night.

> *Ustashe, Ustashe*
> *A deep pit awaits you:*
> *Its width is one metre*
> *Its depth one kilometre ...*

The guards drank. The first 'sacrifices' were brought out —
followed by the sounds of beatings, the screams of the victims, and
the torturers' uncontrollable laughter. The 'Turks' who survived
will never forget that St Vitus's Day.

We also had visitors from outside who came into the camp in order
to take their revenge and settle old scores. One day, about sixteen
Chetniks died in the Kozara Mountain while trying to capture
armed groups that were still refusing to surrender. A group of
survivors, led by a tank driver from Orlovci named Zoran Karlica,
arrived at the camp to take their revenge. Karlica entered our room
and asked the people by the door where they were from.

'From Kevljani.' Everyone was suddenly from Kevljani
because everyone knew that we had not resisted, and it was
therefore the safest place to be from.

Without explaining who he was, or why he was here, Karlica
shouted: 'All men who possessed guns stand up!' Everyone
remained nailed to the floor. He went berserk and threatened all of
us.

'Shall I stand up?' Kasim asked me. I was petrified. He was
scared, too. I could not say a word. Somebody had to stand up, so
Kasim did.

'Tell him you only had a legal automatic pistol,' I whispered
while he was getting up. From the other part of the room, closer to
the door, my old schoolmate Damir stood up, too. A few more
people followed. Karlica asked them what kind of weapons they
had owned.

'Legal pistols,' they said.

'Show me your permits.' Kasim explained he had already
handed it in on Monday, May 25. Karlica did not accept this. He
was not interested in weapons, legal or illegal. He had come to
seek revenge.

'You are a liar,' he said to Damir, belting him across his face.

Damir fell on the floor. Blood poured from his nose.

Karlica then pulled out his pistol and hit Hamdija Balic on the forehead. Blood flowed down Hamdija's face in huge spurts. At this point, a guard named Jovan, who had let Karlica in, told him to stop. But he made no actual effort to prevent him. Only when Pirvan entered and told him to stop did Karlica actually leave — moving on to repeat the same performance in other rooms.

A few days later, another group of soldiers came to the camp for some 'fun'. They weren't looking for anyone in particular. It was evident that in their eyes we were all guilty of something — no matter who we were. One of them, Prevara, a local character, was hitting everybody over the head and the back with a mountaineer's axe. When we returned from our meal, he came to the door of our room. Zaim Klipic, a young man from my village, went to talk to him. Kasim said: 'We used to be colleagues. I'm going to talk to him, too.'

'Don't be a fool. Stay where you are. You used to know him, you don't know him now.' Kasim took my advice.

When outside visitors came looking for a specific target, those left alive after their departure would wonder what might happen on the next such occasion — and whether next time they would be one of the chosen. The most appalling of these orgies happened around June 17. It was late afternoon. Terrible screams penetrated the walls of our room. They could be heard in every corner of the camp. They were screams of fear and of great pain. My hair stood on end. All talk inside the room died out. The screams were mixed with laughter: obviously somebody was being tortured. Only later did we hear what had happened.

Several outside visitors had gone to the two rooms next to the garage. They called out Enver 'Eno' Alic, Jasmin 'Jasko' Hrnic, and Emir 'Karaba' Karabasic. Eno's father Meho was taken to the garage to find his son and bring him out. When the beating started, he could not bear to watch his son being tortured — and he left without asking for permission.

At least two other inmates had been forced to take part in this brutal game. One of them, E. J., a young boy from the northern part of my village, had been ordered to drink motor oil — both from a ditch running through the garage and from a beer bottle given to him by one of the Chetniks. He was then ordered to kneel before Eno Alic, and they forced him to bite off his testicles.

The Chetniks experimented with all kinds of cruelties which arose from a sickened mind, but the nightmare of this particular cruelty will never end for the boy who was made to carry it out. Eno died in terrible agony, but at least it was swift. E. J. will have to live with this horror for the rest of his life. For the Chetniks, it had all been great fun.

Back in his room, E. J. remained in a state of shock for days. Jasko and Karaba had also been killed.

7

The early transaction we had made with 'Cvitonja' Pavlic — food for money — gave the Chetniks the idea to organise a business selling biscuits and cigarettes. They did not deal with us directly. Offering certain incentives, they had recruited several inmates to do this job. I called them traders. Six men from my village became champions of the trade. Five of them operated on the floor where I was kept, and the sixth one covered the two rooms next to the garage. The remaining volunteers operated elsewhere in the camp. From their initial sales activities, their function gradually expanded to organising the groups for meals and toilets. They believed that in this way they were improving their chances of survival. But when their behaviour began to transgress certain boundaries, I found their actions unacceptable. One of them had renounced his own brother.

'I don't have a brother in here. I'm the only one whose life matters.' He told me this in the presence of my own brother —

while his brother was behind the door on the other side of the corridor. He expected me to agree with him. I loved my brother. I wasn't glad that we both had to suffer — but I was glad I was not alone. This particular trader would have exchanged his brother for a couple of biscuits and a cigarette or two.

The garage trader started buying gold from people with whom he had shared a room. They were prepared to sell it for just one pack of cigarettes and a pack of biscuits, which were worth more than gold as gold could be neither eaten nor smoked. As a former employee of the mine, he knew some of the guards well. He had spent a lot of time in their company sharing their rations and making deals. While the rest of us wasted away, he was gaining weight. Not even the fact that his mother was held amongst the women inside the administration building — or that his father was recovering from a wound inflicted by a Chetnik bullet — could prevent him from exploiting the situation. He became one of them. Many other prisoners were enraged by his conduct, but he did not give a damn. He even went as far as signing a contract with one of the other inmates trading a plot of land in exchange for some biscuits and cigarettes. However absurd it may sound, the contract was signed in the presence of witnesses on the back of a biscuit box! It was a clever deal because he knew he wasn't going to be going back home.

By co-operating with the guards, the traders earned a few cigarettes and a little bit of food. If they were careless in their conduct, they could have faced dire consequences. Asim 'Ako' Jakupovic became involved early on in the sale of biscuits and cigarettes. He spent a lot of time in the guards' room. In the end, he started behaving very strangely.

'I don't want to be with these extremists any more. I don't belong in here,' he cried. 'I should have been transferred to Trnopolje.' One night when Pirvan's shift was on duty, Pirvan said: 'This singer is beginning to annoy me. And he knows too much.'

They took Ako outside and started beating him. He was crying: 'Don't kill me. Don't make my children orphans.' He managed to escape upstairs and hide inside one of the smaller rooms opposite the guards' room. The following night, he was taken out again. He died because he had broken the basic camp rule. He had not kept a low profile.

While we had some money, Kasim and I had additional food and cigarettes. From the very beginning we got used to rationing. Five hundred grams of biscuits could last up to five days — two or three biscuits per day. Asim Hodza had some money, too, and before he went for interrogation we had shared everything. After he left, another Asim, Asim M. J., asked us to allow him to stay with us. He knew Kasim, for they sometimes worked together on the same construction sites. He was hard up from the start, but for as long as we had something to eat, he ate too.

Some inmates were too selfish to notice anybody around them. What they bought they would consume without offering anything to the others. Kasim and I were surrounded by neighbours and friends. We didn't have much, but from time to time we offered them as much as we could afford.

When the money was almost gone, Hamdija Jakupovic asked Kasim and me to make some space for him, too. People were disappearing from the room and it became possible to do as he asked. The guards and the outside 'visitors' frequently stormed into the room to beat us, and those closer to the door were more likely to become their victims. Hamdija wanted to move away from that dangerous spot. He still had some money, and he suggested that we pool everything we had. He himself was a bit like Kasim: he could not control his spending. He thought I'd better take care of the money, and make all the decisions about what and when to buy. In this situation I managed our resources to the point where they couldn't be stretched any further.

Some wanted to eat and smoke as much as they had done in

normal circumstances. This quickly left them with nothing. A pack of cigarettes lasted about three days. When money started running out, the three of us would share half a cigarette. We were hungry all the time, yet we smoked rather than spending all the money on food. Only when I had a second or two to think consciously about my hunger did I realise what a torment it was to be fed just enough to keep you alive for another day — a torment which nevertheless led slowly towards certain death. In such moments, my empty stomach would almost make me cry. But at those times when we had to listen to the screams of people being tortured, a cigarette helped more than food. Those were the times when you would forget everything else and wish only for the guards to keep as far away from you as possible. You just wanted to stay alive. Those were the moments when we felt most vulnerable — when we were reminded overwhelmingly of our helplessness.

Nenad 'Neso' Panic, a guard, and Rade Gruban — a person not directly connected with the running of the camp but with great influence amongst those who did — conducted the business on the Serb side. Neso led the group of guards who had all enjoyed torturing Azur Jakupovic, and for many an evening Neso's voice could be heard from the 'White House': 'Azureeee. Where are you, Azureeee?' With the first signs of darkness, the screams coming from the 'White House' echoed throughout the camp.

During the 1980s, Neso had run a successful café in Kozarac. His business had thrived. Traditionally, when the Muslims of Kozarac celebrated *Ramazan Bajram*, a festival that follows the last day of Ramadan and which lasts for three days, Neso was regularly invited to attend the festivities. In those days, Muslims and Serbs of the region respected each other's religious festivities. But that was all in the past. Now, Neso's former hosts could only fear him.

The profits that Neso had made in Kozarac gave him the

opportunity to open his own grocery shop in Omarska. Ironically, in the camp, Muslims of the Kozarac region were once more his most 'loyal' customers.

Rade Gruban was a former ambulance driver. He must have been in his late forties or early fifties. In the late 1980s, he had combined his driving activity with running a small grocery shop in Omarska. Once the camp was open, Rade became its regular 'visitor'.

Inside the camp, Rade liked two things best — selling biscuits and cigarettes, and conducting choral singing of Serbian nationalistic songs. The camp offered him a unique opportunity to express his artistic talent. He chose a number of inmates from the 'White House' to form a choir. Day after day, Maestro Rade visited the camp to arrange the choir rehearsals. He had cultivated a special love for the Chetnik movement that had massacred tens of thousands of non-Serbs during the Second World War. Draza Mihailovic, the infamous leader of this equally infamous movement, had paid for his crimes almost fifty years earlier. But admirers like Rade made sure that the memory of their leader had been kept alive by younger generations. In Draza's honour, the choir rehearsals included songs celebrating Draza and Greater Serbia. At first Rade thought the choir displayed a lack of enthusiasm. The volume of the voices was somehow too low, and the Maestro demanded a bit more effort.

'Can it be louder? I want to hear it. Louder, louder.' And so the grandchildren of Draza's victims sang:

> *From Topola, from Topola*
> *All the way to Ravna Gora,*
> *All the guards are,*
> *All the guards are*
> *General Draza's ...*

Hearing these tunes regularly, I came to learn them myself. When a group of Serbian leaders from Banja Luka led by Predrag Radic, Banja Luka's mayor and the president of the Serbian Democratic Party (SDS) for Bosnian Krajina, arrived at the camp, the choir and the Maestro were ready for their first public performance. The choir, lined up by the proud Maestro, held a Serbian flag. They greeted Radic and his delegation with one loud: 'Welcome to Greater Serbia!'

Rising to the occasion, Radic replied with the well-known Chetniks' salute: 'God bless you heroes.'

'God bless you,' they responded.

'One, two, three ...' Cutting the air with his hands, Maestro Rade gave a signal to the choir to raise three fingers signifying the Holy Trinity in the Serbian Orthodox church — a symbol of Serb nationalists. We were all ears. The choir sang:

> *Who is it telling lies that*
> *Serbia is small?*
> *She is not small, she is not small.*
> *Three times she fought in a war.*
>
> *She'll fight again, and again,*
> *She won't be a slave.*
> *She'll fight again, and again,*
> *She won't be a slave ...*

The choir gave their best performance. Rade was proud that they had not let him down. They could not have afforded to disappoint him. Later on, the Maestro and the choir had several more opportunities to perform for groups of Serbian high military officials. Unfortunately, some members of the choir 'disappeared' between the visits. They were replaced with fresh talent.

When Emso Softic, one of the lead singers, was singled out for a beating, it took place on the grass in front of the 'White House'. While raining blows on him with a truncheon, a guard called him a 'dirty Turk'.

'What are you?' the guard shouted — expecting him to say a 'dirty Turk'.

'A Serb!' yelled Emso.

'You lying Turkish bastard — what are you?'

'A Serb!'

'Since when?'

'Since I was born!'

'I'll — break — your — fucking — Turkish — neck,' the guard was saying as he whacked Emso rhythmically. 'Since when are you a Serb?'

'Since today!' yelled Emso.

'That's better', said the guard. 'Well, Serb, which is your Saints' Day?'

'St George!'

'When is St George's Day?'

'The sixth of May!'

The guard stopped beating him. He turned to the other guards, laughing: 'Did you hear that? The motherfucker knows the date, too!' And he let the 'convert' go.

The choir rehearsals were usually scheduled for the afternoon, but the Grubans proved to be a very musical family. The Maestro's younger son, Goran, a camp guard, confirmed that an apple does not fall far from the tree. The choir was already well-trained, and Goran decided to experiment with his style of music.

Rade's repertoire clearly showed his preference for the more traditional style of Serbian music — the one that celebrated the old Serbian 'glory', the time when Serb army recruits traditionally came from peasant and mountain stock. Goran, however, seemed to admire the new Chetnik style — embodied by Arkan's 'Tigers' and Bokan's 'White Eagles'. They had Western tastes — green camouflage fatigues, berets, and expensive sunglasses or balaclavas. During the Second World War, Rade's Chetniks looked more like shepherds dressed to scare wolves away from their flocks of sheep. They wore black sheepskin hats, had long unkempt hair, moustaches and long, unkempt beards, and carried two rounds of ammunition strapped across their chests — a costume daunting enough to make even grizzlies run away.

The choir's timetable was now full. In the morning, immediately after the shift change, rehearsals began with Goran. In the afternoon, sometimes before a meal, sometimes after a meal, and sometimes with no meal at all (it all depended when the yellow lorry brought food to the camp), there would be rehearsals with Rade.

Under Goran's baton, the choir would sing verses to the tune of the familiar chant of the US Marines:

> *There are no guards*
> *without kokards,*[1]
> *There are no soldiers*
> *but the Chetniks...*

This song was just the warm-up. Goran was pleased with the choir's performance. They seemed to have an ear for both the tune and the lyrics. After some time, another song would begin:

> *One morning at dawn*
> *A Serb fucked a Muslim woman...*

Goran was young. He had just turned twenty. Many years lay ahead of him — for his father preferred not to run the risk of

---

1. The *Kokarda* is an insignia featuring a double-headed eagle, traditionally worn by the Chetniks.

sacrificing such profound musical talent by allowing Goran to join his idols in combat. Let them get on with their job, and he would promote their glory with his music.

In the afternoon, his father would arrive at the camp.

'Hi son. How did it go?'

'Fine, Dad. Fine.'

'Good. OK, my nightingales — let's hear my favourite one.'
Rade's nightingales began to sing:

> *From Topola, from Topola*
> *All the way to Ravna Gora,*
> *All the guards are,*
> *All the guards are*
> *General Draza's...*

8

Strange as it may seem, my memories of the camp do not consist only of horror stories. Sometimes I remember that time not just with bitterness, but with a smile.

The inmates kept in the same room with me never seemed to run out of words. Our 'living quarters' were like a beehive. One of the topics which could never be exhausted was food. Meals and dishes which mothers and wives used to make were described and compared in the smallest detail by people grinning from ear to ear.

The only cooking experience which most of us had had was preparing scrambled eggs or instant soup. Suddenly, fifty per cent of the inmates found a piece of paper somewhere — a piece of biscuit box or even paper from a cigarette pack — and with a borrowed pen started writing down recipes. Room 24 produced small recipe books. For a short time, the inmates were able to push aside the brutal reality with their enthusiasm for new culinary discoveries. Even those of us who had no ambitions to become famous chefs when freed got conscripted into the activity. The enthusiasts pestered us to dictate to them whatever we could recall of favourite recipes from home.

I liked the stories of the summer holidays Hamdija used to spend in Macedonia, where he had family. The Macedonian Mediterranean climate was perfect for growing different kinds of fruit — especially peaches, watermelons and grapes. At the time of his visits, most of them were ready for picking. Back in Bosnia we fought the heat with a cold drink, but his family in Macedonia would drink hot tea — a kind of tea so strong it could leave you feeling drunk. I visited Hamdija's Macedonia in my daydreams, indulging in food and drink, sunbathing, and listening to stories told by Hamdija and his cousins. They laughed and I laughed with them.

Sometimes I visited Emir in another part of the room, closer to the door. He was there with some men from Kozarac, and occasionally I would take two cigarettes and some biscuits and go to talk with him. Spending time with Emir, I had a chance to talk to the people around him. I liked the way they talked about food. I liked their optimism for life.

One of them had a great passion for orchards. He cultivated rare fruits that were on the verge of extinction. Everybody preferred the new hybrid types, but he knew the new hybrids had none of the beauty of the old fruit. The new fruits were big and had monotonous colours — yellow, dark red, green. The old sorts offered a whole variety of colours, and were juicier and tasted much better. His talk about his fruit trees and the ripe fruit — including his vineyard's delicious grapes — could only be compared to a passionate lover adoring his woman.

This same man, Salih, had another great passion. He enjoyed spending weekends in the hills above his house. Coming home after Friday's work, he would put his knapsack on and go off to enjoy the fresh mountain air and the smells of wild flowers growing in the meadows. For many years, he used the same footpath on his way to the upper parts of the mountain, passing by an old linden tree. He never paid much attention to this tree. It was just an old and tired tree. And then one summer everything changed. He decided to take a short break, and being close to the tree it seemed a perfect place to rest. As he sat down, he noticed an unusual number of bees flying around. This aroused his curiosity and he took a closer look. To his surprise, bees were coming in and out of the tree trunk.

'Honey!' he thought instantly.

Without wasting time, he smoked the bees out — but he had nothing in which to collect the honey. He wrapped pieces of honeycomb in his jacket. He returned home with his honey-filled jacket and headed back up the path with a friend and a chainsaw, determined to collect the rest. They cut the tree down and found more than twenty kilograms of honey. They should have left something for the bees, but the excitement of the discovery left them unable to think about anything else. The old tree that had been a good host and a home for the bees certainly deserved to remain upright. That way all the parties would have been happy. The bees would still have had a home in the tree, and the men would have had a fruitful harvest for many years to come. But when kids find honey they forget everything else, and that afternoon these two men were the biggest kids in the world.

Even though it was a sad ending for the bees and the old tree, I enjoyed the story very much. Back at my place on the other side of the room, I replayed the whole event in my head. I stood in the meadows observing their every move — shouting to them to spare the tree that had stood there for decades, defying the brisk mountain winds and harsh, chilly winters — the tree that contained wisdom and memories of past times. But they could not hear me. They were children in paradise.

I had always dreamt of starting my own orchard and keeping my own bees.

9

I always tried to be invisible — but my unusually long hair was my downfall. It drew attention to me. I was abused verbally, hit with rifles, and threatened with scalping. Pirvan, the shift leader on my floor, was a man with an icy smile which suggested evil and created fear. He did not always smile either. Noko, a young boy from my village, once saw him stabbing a man from Prijedor. I always tried to avoid Pirvan's cold smile, but this was not always possible as he noticed my long hair. One evening when it was just about time for the guards to close the door, I rushed to the entrance asking Jovan, another guard, to let me use the toilet. I had stomach cramps.

'Why didn't you use it when everybody else did?' he asked. 'You see, it's time to mop the corridor.' Samir, one of the 'traders' who had been assigned cleaning duties, stood there holding a mop and a bucket.

'The pain started just a minute ago. When I come back I'll help with the cleaning.'

After a little hesitation, he let me out. 'All right,' he said, 'but don't take too long.'

'I won't.' I ran towards the toilet.

I tried hard to be quick. I was afraid a guard might come and ask what I was doing there. I gave up. I tried to sneak back to my room.

'Hey, you. Where do you think you're going?' Jovan had spotted me from the guards' room.

I quickly grabbed a mop and a bucket and started cleaning the corridor. Moments later, with his usual icy smile, Pirvan came out of the guardroom and asked: 'How's it going?'

'All right.' I looked up briefly and continued working.

'Are you a musician? Do you write music?' He kept smiling.

'No, I don't.' I tried to sound calm to hide my anxiety.

'Do you play a guitar?' Maybe he wanted me to entertain them, I thought.

'No, I don't.'

'Didn't you tour Germany with your group?'

'I just like to listen to music. That's all I have to do with music.'

'Just like to listen to music, eh?'

'That's right.'

'Get on with it.' He went back to the guardroom.

Samir later told me that while I had been in the toilet, Pirvan had asked him: 'Do you know this guy?'

'Yes I do. He's from my village.'

'What's he like?'

'He's a good guy,' Samir replied.

From this moment, Pirvan never forgot my face. He never asked for my name. From then on he called me a 'musician'. This was dangerous.

I hated any encounter with the guards. Every eye contact was filled with fear. Every verbal communication further deepened this fear. But sometimes, circumstances forced me to initiate contact with them for reasons stronger than fear.

A few days later, the soup had a bit of meat in it — it was too tough to chew. I put it into my piece of bread and took it back to my room. While I was trying to eat it, my next-door neighbour Crni laughed.

'Kemo, is it good?' He was teasing me because I was a vegetarian.

'It's lovely,' I said. Everybody around me burst into loud laughter.

After midnight, I felt the first stomach cramps. I stood up in the hope that the pain would soon go away, but it was getting worse. My movements woke up Kasim.

'What's wrong?' he asked.

'I have terrible cramps in my stomach. I have to go to the toilet.'

'You'd better wait until morning.' The guards never let anyone use the toilet after 7.30pm. He was worried that going out this late was far too dangerous. But the pain was tearing my stomach apart. I could not bear it any more.

'I'm going to knock on the door,' I said. The pain was stronger than fear. 'The pain is unbearable.' He said nothing.

I walked through the darkness trying to avoid stepping on men who were attempting to catch some sleep. I reached the door and knocked quietly. When it opened I felt a kind of relief. I saw a familiar face. Zoran 'Djaja' Romanic was sitting behind it. He was a postman, and for several years he had delivered mail to my village. Because I was not standing, but crouching, he asked: 'What's wrong?'

'I have to go to the toilet. My stomach is killing me.'

'Can you wait until morning?'

'No, I can't. I have to go now.'

'All right,' he said, looking down the corridor to make sure no-one else was there. 'But be quiet and quick. Don't stay too long.'

I ran down the corridor as fast as I could — not only because he told me to be quick, but also because I was not sure I would reach the toilet on time. The pain had become real agony. Thousands of knives were tearing me apart. A cold wave struck my head and neck, followed by temporary blindness. I was panicking.

When I felt a bit better, I hurried back to the room. In seventy-three days, I had emptied my bowels three times.

Inside the room, Sero waited at the door, wracked with the same problem. I came in and he went out. Back at my place, I tried to sleep — but a few minutes later, the pains started all over again. Before Sero was back, the door opened and a guard called Zdravko Govedarica asked: 'Is Sero Velic in here?' Somebody next to the door replied: 'He just went to the toilet.'

A minute or two later, Sero opened the door and set down a canister he had filled with tap water. He closed the door and remained outside.

Meanwhile, men from all over the room were getting up and running towards the door, seized by the same acute stomach pain. The running up and down the corridor lasted until six o'clock in the morning. I had to go back to the toilet six times.

Around 5.00am, Govedarica brought Sero back. He was naked above the waist. Govedarica just threw him inside the room. Sero collapsed on to the floor. He wept quietly — asking for help. But everybody was too scared to approach him. A tall man from Kozarusa finally got up and had a look at him. Only then did other men follow. They tried to take Sero back to his usual place, but he yelled out in pain. He had been beaten severely from head to foot. There was not a single spot untouched. Several ribs had been broken. They put him into a blanket and tried to carry him. Every little movement made him cry out. Finally, a space was made for him close to the door.

Three hours earlier, he had been taken to one of the interrogation offices. Govedarica had offered him some *sljivovica* — a plum brandy. Milojica 'Krle' Kos then asked him, 'Why didn't you offer some *sljivovica* to Baja and me when we came to your house last summer?' Baja Beric was a policeman from Omarska.

The previous summer, Sero had lent them some of his tractor equipment. When they brought the equipment back a couple of days later, he had been very busy. In this rush, he had neglected to offer them a drink — which was customary, but not obligatory. Now Krle was remembering this slight. Instead of being grateful to him for the favour he had shown them, they had taken offence at not having been offered a drink. Krle, Govedarica and their gang then accused Sero of organising 'defence' in our village, and of co-operating with 'defence organisers' in other Muslim villages in the area. They addressed him as 'Captain'. He was ordered to take off everything but his underwear. He had to lie on the tiled floor and to straighten his limbs as much as possible. He was made ready for torture. They beat him with rifle butts along the spine and the ribcage. Whips and truncheons were applied elsewhere. He was also kicked in the groin. He lost consciousness several times. Buckets of water stood nearby, prepared in advance, to bring him back to life. One of the questions he was most frequently asked was: 'Where is the Breda machine gun?' This was the first time in my life I had heard of such a weapon. There had never been such a gun in the village. He was beaten like this for three hours. When he was brought back to our room, the only help we could provide was a cold compress.

Coincidentally, the next morning an army ambulance arrived with an army doctor — a Colonel by rank, and two nurses from the Omarska medical centre. They asked if anybody needed medical help. People with sore throats got some penicillin pills, and those wounded earlier had their wounds bandaged. Four people took Sero outside in the blanket. When the doctor saw him, he just said: 'I can't help him. Take him back upstairs very carefully. If you drop him, he won't survive.'

This time they did not bring him back to our room. They took him to the room only recently set aside for the sick. In the following days, Sero just lay there without any medical attention.

Three days later, the ambulance vehicle and its staff disappeared, never to return. Around this time, Vasif Foric started having terrible pains in his right eye. He sat close to Kasim and me. Kasim knew him and asked him about his pain. He said that he felt a burning sensation in his eye. He had no painkillers or anything else to mitigate his suffering. The only help he could get was a wet handkerchief applied to his eye. He never complained — he just kept quiet. But the agonising pain he suffered could be seen in his other eye. Looking at this eye sent cold shivers down my spine. After a while, the pain stopped, and Vasif felt a bit better — but not for very long. The pain came back with a vengeance. His inflamed eye turned red, and soon after that it was coated with a white film. He had one white, blind eye. Had the doctor remained in the camp, he may have been able to save it.

The worst threats to life were constant beatings, starvation and the total lack of hygienic conditions. The only sources of drinking water were the taps in the toilets and in the sinks. This water was heavily contaminated with iron-ore particles. After it was left to stand in a plastic bottle, there would be reddish sediment at the bottom. This water came from the river, which had been used for years in the process of purifying the iron ore from the soil. But it was the only water we had. There were frequent power cuts, and we remained thirsty for hours. Later on, somebody realised that during these cuts, water from the hydrant outside the building could be used. This was even worse. It was supplied directly from the river, and there was a risk of hepatitis and typhoid. However, it was either this water or dehydration.

Hygiene did not exist as such. There were no bathing facilities. Nothing to wash your hands with in the toilet. We were steadily becoming filthy. Heat, sweat, no change of clothes. Twice we were ordered by the guards to move outside and 'bathe'. We formed ourselves into groups of fifty. The first group stood on the grass below the 'White House' while Pirvan simply hosed them down with a huge hose. The jet of water was so strong that many people fell over. Once 'bathing' was finished they put their dirty clothes back on again.

I wet my hair and I mixed with the group that had just had the 'bath'. The guards did not notice. They were standing around laughing, watching the spectacle. Many of the inmates could hardly contain their excitement as they waited their turn. They were like children anticipating their first dip in the sea. Some were even laughing together with the guards.

Throughout the entire period of my detention, I wore the same clothes. After some time, my clothes and I became so filthy, I smelt like a rat. It was particularly bad during hot days, and the summer of 1992 was very hot. Kasim once spread his jeans on a wall to dry off the sweat. Next morning, they were so stiff with sweat and dirt that he could stand them up.

We were all growing beards and long hair. Day by day, our hair became greasier and dirtier. I combed mine every day — and more and more of it was falling out. Then one day, to our surprise, my neighbour Fajko came for a visit from the garage bringing a razor. Somebody had smuggled it into the camp. Fajko's razor was anything but sharp. God knows how many other beards it had shaved before reaching us. Even though the blade was already worn out, Fajko managed to shave some thirty of us — even though he was just wetting our beards and pulling out hairs rather than shaving them.

The place bred all sorts of vermin, lice and fleas. Combing lice out of our hair turned into a sort of entertainment. Counting them and measuring whose were bigger and fatter became a sort of competition. The fleas were much better fed than we were. They would jump with an incredible speed.

When the beatings started to increase in ferocity, many of those around me became afraid to go to the toilet. Instead, they started using one of the sinks. One morning the sink was overflowing.

'Is there anyone else in there who wants to go out to the grass?' Jovan's voice was calling from the door.

'Yes, there is.' I needed some fresh air.

'Don't go out,' Kasim was saying behind me. 'Use the sink.'

'No, I want to go out,' I snapped. I hated the horrible smell of excrement that spread from the sink. The trouble was, nobody else wanted to go out and I didn't know this. I stepped out of the room and was promptly slapped.

'Why didn't you say earlier that you needed to go out?' Apparently, he'd asked the same question before.

'I'm staying in the showers. It's a bit isolated from the rest of the room. I didn't hear you,' I was saying as I dodged the blows. Pirvan stood next to him.

'OK, OK, leave him alone. Musician, are you all right?' he asked, laughing. I was boiling inside, but did not dare to show it. I even tried to make a friendly face.

'Run outside now. You have four minutes to come back.' Jovan looked like a raging bull with angry steam coming through his nostrils. I was turning to run down the stairs when Pirvan shouted: 'Wait. Let him go to one of these two.' He pointed with his head towards the two toilets next to the stairs. 'There's nobody in there now.'

I slipped inside the first one. I tried not to stay a second longer than necessary. On my way back, Pirvan said: 'All right?'

While all this was happening, those sitting next to the door could see everything. By the time I was back at my shower cabin,

Inmates at Omarska jog across the yard and eat in the cafeteria. While they were forced to present a false picture of the camp to journalists, we were hidden from view.

My class at the local school. I am standing in the back row, sixth from right. The drawing illustrates the devastating effect the war had on my friends, classmates and the village community in general.

1. FAHRUDIN SIVAC
   Currently in Slovenia. One of his brothers disappeared in Omarska, another was killed in the war.

2. His father, OSMAN KARABASIC and brother DEDO both survived Omarska, but were killed on a convoy travelling through Central Bosnia.

3. DZEVAD MURIC
   Killed in fighting in Central Bosnia.

4. MILAN MILUTINOVIC
   A Serb that Kemal spotted at Omarska. He was not a guard.

5. DAMIR HADZIC
   Survived Omarska. His brother was killed by Croats in 1993.

6. His father, MUSTAFA PERVANIC was taken off the convoy in Central Bosnia by Serbs and killed.

7. MILOJICA BERIC
   A Serbian guard at Omarska.

8. His brothers, MEDO HADZIC and ILIJAZ disappeared in Omarska.

9. SMAIL KEVAC
   Now lives in France. He survived Omarska and Manjaca.

10. Her husband ASIM 'AKO' JAKUPOVIC was killed in Omarska, her brother RASIM HODZIC was taken from the convoy in Central Bosnia and killed.

11. SENAD SIVAC
    Killed at Omarska the day before the transfer to Manjaca.

12. Her brother MEHEMED JAKUPOVIC was killed in Omarska.

13. Her brother, BAKIR JAKUPOVIC was killed in Omarska.

14. Her two brothers-in-law, MUHAREM and MIRALEM IBRAHIMOVIC were both killed in Trnopolje.

15. Her husband and father-in-law were killed in their village.

16. Brother ALEM 'ACO' JAKUPOVIC was killed in Omarska.

17. MIRZET SIVAC disappeared during an attack on the village.

18. KEMAL PERVANIC
    Survived Omarska and the transfer to Manjača. Now lives in the UK.

IV/2

NO. CICR: ...0.0.2.0.9.3.5.0....

CARTE D'IDENTIFICATION

LIČNA/OSOBNA KARTA

A CONSERVER PAR LE TITULAIRE

ČUVATI SA SOBOM

NOM DE FAMILLE/
PREZIME: ..PERVANIC..............

PRENOM/
IME: ....KEMAL..................

LIEU NAISSANCE/
MESTO/MJESTO ROĐENJA: ....
KEVLJANI   PRIJEDOR   BiH
....

DATE NAISSANCE/
DATUM ROĐENJA: .09.04.1968.

16.12.1992.

20.12.shoes
27.12.92. F
3.1.93

M.1. Jaket+Hat

11.1.F

17.1.F

20 12 1992

079   11-137   42

N.1. N5

The registration card that I was given by the IRC on arrival at Manjaca. It was a
tremendous relief, as it seemed that it would be hard for the Serbs to dispose of us if
we had been registered.

This is the message that I received from my brother Asim while at Manjaca. It was the first confirmation I had that my family were still alive. It reads:

**Hello brother,
Our old man and I are alright. Mother arrived and is here with us in Zagreb. She is alright. Many greetings from us.**

---

7.   ЧСК   MESSAGE CROIX - ROUGE
     100   PORUKA CRVENOC KRSTA
     2.9.92   за МЧСК PORUKA CRVENOG KRIŽA

8. EXPEDITEUR / POŠILJALAC / POŠILJJALAC   No. CICR ....

Nom complet (selon l'usage local)
Puno ime i prezime
Puno ime i prezime   PERVANIĆ ASIM

Date de naissance 4.4.1960   Sexe : (M) / F
Datum rodjenja   Pol : M / 2
Datum rodjenja   Spol : M / 2

Nom complet du père PERVANIĆ SMAIL
Puno ime i prezime oca / Puno ime i prezime oca

Adresse postale complète   Code postal ....
Puna postanska adresa / Puna adresa stanovanja Postanski broj
ZASTAVNICA BB   Postanski broj

41421 HRVATSKI LESKOVAC   Telephone ....
    ZAGREB HRVATSKA   Telefon / Telefon

9. DESTINATAIRE / PRIMALAC / PRIMATELJ   No. CICR ....

Nom complet (selon l'usage local)
Puno ime i prezime
Puno ime i prezime   KEMAL PERVANIĆ

Date de naissance   Sexe : M / F
Datum rodjenja   Pol : M / 2
Datum rodjenja   Spol : M / 2

Nom complet du père SMAIL PERVANIĆ
Puno ime i prezime oca / Puno ime i prezime oca

Adresse postale complète   Code postal ....
Puna postanska adresa / Puna adresa stanovanja Postanski broj
MANJACA   Postanski broj

78000 BANA LU...

10.

     COMITE INTERNAT...
     MEDUNARODNI ...

     19. av. de la ...

---

11.   REPONSE   AU   MESSAGE
             ODGOVOR   NA   PORUKU
     (Nouvelles de caractère personnel et/ ou familial)
              (Vesti lične i / ili porodične prirode)
           (Poruka osobne i / ili porodične prirode)

ZDRAVO BURAZ JA I STARI
SMO DOBRO MATI JE POSLA
KOD NAS U ZAGREB. ONA
JE DOBRO.
PUNO POZDRAVA OD NAS.

12.
Date
Datum 25.9.1992   Signature Pervanić Asim
Datum   Potpis
                     Potpis

My brother Kasim at the Red Cross Centre flat in Newcastle shortly after our parents'
arrival in the UK. He is now staying in Holland.

Top: My mother in my parents' flat in Newcastle.

Bottom: My elder brother Asim, me and my father. This was taken in Scotland. All my family, bar Kasim, now live in the UK.

As I appeared two months after leaving Manjaca, still a little thin.

Kasim already knew what had happened.

'Didn't I tell you not to go out? But you don't listen to me.'

After this incident, and after often seeing people beaten much more badly than I had been, I joined the club and used the sink every time the guards from this shift were on duty. Many of those previously beaten did not dare to go out at all. During power cuts, five hundred men would block the sink with excrement in two or three hours. Some men walked around with dirt on their trousers. They did not have enough strength to wash it off. It wasn't our full stomachs, but rather our sick bodies which had made this mess unavoidable. When dysentery started raging, the four-metre-long sink was permanently topped with excrement. No words in this world could describe the stench spreading around the room. While excrement and urine floated in the sink, some people had to sleep beneath it overnight, and sit leaning against it during the day.

This was the time when many people became seriously ill. Everybody was becoming weak through slow starvation, and blood pressure was dropping to dangerously low levels. Those with high blood pressure and diabetes did not survive long. Every time I stood up I had blackouts. Inside the room, I could cope with it. But on the way to the canteen it was dangerous. Once, on the way to the canteen, my legs suddenly went rubbery, and I kept expecting to fall down. Images of the Chetniks and of the men in front of me blurred and then completely disappeared. Pitch darkness enveloped me, turning into a white vacuum. Voices around me were silenced.

'It can't be real, it can't be real,' I was telling myself. I was frightened to death. 'I can't see where I'm going. If I stray away from the others they'll kill me.' I quickly said to Kasim: 'I can't see or hear anything.' He grabbed my hand and dragged me to the canteen.

My eyes were wide open, but I could see nothing. I could

speak but could not hear Kasim reply. In the canteen, he took plates with food for both of us. I did not eat. I did not know where my plate was.

'I need just a couple of seconds and this will pass,' I said to Kasim. 'You eat my soup and take the bread with you.'

He knew we had no time to wait. He did not listen to me, but instead guided my hand and I started to eat. When pictures and voices inside the canteen started to reappear, I noticed that others were already getting up from the tables. I quickly began to swallow the rest of the beans without chewing them. I had not yet finished all of my portion, when a passing inmate who had eaten the last of his meagre helping and was on his way out of the canteen spotted a rare chance to help himself to a bit of extra soup from a weakened prisoner's plate. He dived at my plate with a spoon, but Kasim brushed him aside and allowed me to take in a bit more of our daily slop.

I was lucky. This frightening weakness did not happen again. Day after day following this experience, I was once again able to keep running to the canteen.

Some older men were weakened to the point where they could no longer stand on their feet. Smail Garibovic was a middle-aged man from my village whose quiet character remains imprinted on my memory. Those who knew him better said he suffered from severe blood-pressure disorders. Every day he would gaze in my direction with his mouth wide open, as if he wanted to say 'help' but did not have enough strength to say it. No words, no sounds, no movements came from him at all. He was a living statue. My eyes met his so many times — but I knew he could not see me. His eyes were lifeless. He no longer knew who he was, or where he was. He no longer went to eat. Shortly before his death, he was moved to the room for the sick.

Behind Smail, a few metres further into the sink section, another similar drama was taking place. An old man and his young son kept their tragedy to themselves. I didn't know whether this old man suffered from some terrible disease, or what the nature of his illness was. Watching them day after day, this tragedy affected me more deeply than deaths caused by violence. The father could no longer walk. He had not been beaten by the guards. He just gave up on life. He did not go to eat. Maybe he had had enough of humiliation. Maybe he just wanted to retain some kind of dignity. He lay on the concrete floor, and never spoke. His frail body was turning into a pile of bones. The shallow breathing movements of his abdomen were the only remaining signs of life.

His son sat next to him, looking like his father's guardian. His eyes said, 'Don't come close. Don't touch him. Don't try to take him away.' His eyes declared that he was ready to defend his father's right to die in peace. The same eyes were saying that deep down he was crying for his father, but they never shed a tear. Other people sat around the two men, but all lines of communication had been cut. Father and son were there in the same room with the rest of us, but at the same time worlds away.

Some inmates began to call the old man the 'Ethiopian'. They still carried with them images of the famine that had devastated Ethiopia in the 1980s. They did not realise that soon many of them would become 'Ethiopians' themselves.

The old man died. His son remained alone. His grief was too great. He became further engulfed in his loneliness.

There were many others who died quietly. They are not remembered as often as those who died violently. But the deaths of Smail and 'Ethiopian' were violent in their own way.

10

The Chetniks extracted a lot of money from us through sales of biscuits and cigarettes. Soon they decided that a simpler way to do it was by threats and by force. The first such experience came when Dalija Hrnjak from Kozarac, who was held in the same room with me, broke a toilet bowl by accident. The Chetniks demanded several hundred German marks.

'We need the money to replace the broken bowl with a new one,' Pirvan said to us.

We had no choice but to collect the money. The toilet bowl was never replaced. Soon after, Dalija was stabbed and he died from the wound. This incident had nothing to do with the toilet bowl. He just happened to be in the wrong place at the wrong time. It was raining heavily and he had taken cover in the doorway of the 'White House' at the very moment when some of the inmates of the 'White House' were being killed. He was stabbed practically by accident. The guards probably thought he was one of the

'White House' prisoners. Pirvan later came to our room and apologised. He said that Dalija's stabbing had been a mistake.

A few days later, the same group of guards, led by Pirvan, demanded six thousand German marks. A day or two earlier, sixteen Chetniks had been killed in the Kozara Mountain while trying to capture small groups of armed men who were still refusing to surrender.

'We need money to build them a memorial,' Pirvan said — obviously finding it hard to keep a straight face. They knew we had some money, and they also knew we would deliver it without resistance.

When almost none of us had any money left, the Chetniks adopted a different strategy. A randomly chosen person would be called outside and would return to our room with a small box. Once it was two men from my village, Alija and Abid. They carried two boxes.

'They want us to collect three hundred German marks and ten cigarettes,' they said. This was new. They had never asked for cigarettes before.

'If we don't give them what they want, they said they would beat us up.' But there was no money left. So they failed to deliver and they paid dearly for their failure.

These were typical cases, where no individual was specifically targeted for his own money. But there were also a number of instances where the Chetniks approached a particular person. The selected man was to give them the money they believed he had kept hidden at home.

A wealthy businessman from Kozarac, Hamdija Balic, owned several boutiques across former Yugoslavia. He had been selling clothes designed and made in his own factory. He had also supplied boutiques in the Croatian capital, Zagreb. Being a wealthy person was enough to endanger his life. As a diabetes sufferer, he had been transferred to the sick room. From there, he was taken outside the camp by Milan Andjic, a 'businessman' from Omarska. Rumours circulated that Andjic was the one pulling all the strings in the Omarska camp, and four or five days later Hamdija was back in the sick room. He did not stay there long. He was selected for the exchange of prisoners of war, which was another name for summary execution.

Unlike Hamdija, another wealthy inmate, Nurko Kahrimanovic, managed to survive. Nurko had acquired his wealth by running restaurants. He was personally involved in organising background support for the defence of Kozarac. This fact was well-known to some camp officials. Nurko allegedly knew the place where a hundred and twenty-five automatic rifles had been buried prior to his surrender. He was taken back to Kozarac by the camp authorities to indicate the site of the buried weapons. He was not expected to survive, but he did. Some said he bought his survival by giving the Chetniks a hundred thousand German marks.

There was no logic in it. Hamdija was wealthier than Nurko. He was not involved in secret rifle stores — so where did he fail? His failure and the survival of others was obviously down to pure chance. The game was played according to the rules of Russian roulette.

Kasim and I had very little money with us. One of the early rumours in connection with the interrogations was that everybody was thoroughly searched as interrogators looked for money and jewellery. Sedin and Dido were split from us after our arrival at Omarska, but they knew we had a single thousand German marks note. Our neighbour Fajko soon came from their room and suggested he had better keep it safe for us until after we had been interrogated. It seemed like a good idea, but soon after he took the money we discovered that the rumours were just rumours. Kasim and I wanted the money back, but by now many people had become aware of our note. The risk to us was very high. If the guards learned of the note, Kasim or I or both of us might simply 'disappear' after dark. Once the guards took someone out of our building, he had a very slim chance of coming back. They were prepared to kill for much less than a thousand marks.

Irfo, another neighbour, returned the money to us. I hid it in the safest place I could think of — the double space inside my underpants. It remained there for the next two months. Fearing for our own safety, we never attempted to change the note. We both believed the trouble it would stir up would outweigh any possible benefits.

Those who knew about the money kept coming and asking for a share. Kasim was already in deep trouble because of his rifle, but even those who had mentioned Kasim's name in connection with arms had no hesitation about coming to ask him for money — exposing him to a new danger. Some kept coming to ask for money for themselves, and those less 'courageous' preferred to send a representative on their behalf. It was usually the garage trader. Every time they wanted money, a guard came to the door and asked Kasim to come out and talk to them. The whole course of the conversation took place under the watchful eye and keen ears of a guard. To save his own skin, Kasim had to ask them so many times: 'If I had more money, do you think I would not buy food and cigarettes for myself?'

It was suicidal to say anything else. These men were digging his grave. The fear he felt inside himself became visible only when he was back in our corner. Finally, we got a chance when the guards were not around to tell these people to stop fooling around before it was too late.

I could understand that these were the desperate attempts of hungry people. They were desperate to get some more food. Nevertheless they should have remembered that even in such circumstances it was important to consider the possible threat not only to their own lives, but to the lives of others. It was certainly more painful for Kasim and me than for them to have this money and not to be able to make use of it.

Over time, the members of Krkan's shift exceeded the other two shifts in savagery. The men in his shift were all very young. Everybody inside the camp feared them most. During the nights when they controlled the camp, the most brutal murders took place. Throughout the night, without warning, they would bang with truncheons and iron rods on the metal doors of Rooms 24 and 15 — creating a fearful racket which made the whole camp jump.

'Wakey, wakey,' they yelled in shrill voices.

'Don't sleep, *Balije*.'[2] The voices would come from the garage beneath us. This kept us awake all night. Deep fear would fill the room.

'Whose turn is it now?' We waited in trepidation for them to burst in and take out new victims. 'Will it be me?' This was the question on everyone's mind.

One of the nights when they were on duty, the door opened. The light came on. The first thought I had was: 'What the hell! Not again!' Then a voice from the door asked: 'Where is Kasim Pervanic? I'm looking for Kasim Pervanic.' I froze. I thought it was Kasim's turn.

Then Alem Jakupovic appeared in the showers and my fear abated a little. Still, why this sudden visit in the middle of the night?

For several weeks before this night, Alem had behaved carelessly. He was amongst those who had sent a messenger to Kasim asking for two hundred marks. He probably had more money than us, but he kept buying biscuits and cigarettes at very excessive prices. He was trading without involving a middleman.

Alem was 'friends' with two of the guards. Dusko had worked with him at Banja Luka's paper mill, and Nedeljko Soskan even kept him under his personal protection. Every time they wanted to give him change, he refused to take it.

---

2. *Balije* is a derogatory Serb term for Muslims.

Soon, smoking and eating as if he were not inside the camp inevitably left him with no money. In the end, a disaster befell him. When Soskan found out he had possessed a gun, it completely changed Alem's situation. A neighbour and a life-long friend betrayed him — probably without realising what he was doing. Ziko told Soskan about Alem's gun within range of Sabit's hearing. Sabit told us about it later. It might have been a foolish accident, but what was said could not be retrieved. Those several seconds of Ziko's thoughtlessness had sealed Alem's fate. Soskan's instantaneous reaction was to take Alem out of the room and ask: 'You motherfucker, why didn't you tell me that you had a gun?'

The following day, after midnight, Alem was taken out by an old enemy — another camp guard who bore Alem a grudge from the past. Only Soskan could have saved him from this guard's revenge. But Soskan's protection had vanished. The guards gave Alem a severe beating. They ordered him to collect two thousand German marks. Back in his room, he managed to collect only about six hundred. The guards resumed the beatings with iron rods. He was given a further fifteen minutes to collect more money. Back inside his room, he pleaded: 'Give me a cigarette, please. It's going to be my last one.'

Then he came to our room. 'Kasim, brother,' he said desperately, 'you have to give me the thousand marks you have. They'll kill me. I'll give you back double when we get out.' I unbuttoned my jeans and took the money out. He left the room and a loud exclamation of delight was heard outside. I could recognise that voice among millions of others. I heard blows made with a heavy, blunt object — probably the same iron rod that had made him faint earlier.

Alem did not cry out. A couple of groans was the last we heard of him. The place of his execution and the shower cubicle in which I was staying were divided only by a thin wall.

'How many more times will I have to see familiar faces

disappearing for ever?' I asked myself, more in anger than in sadness.

I was a changed person. It seemed to me that living inside a slaughterhouse had made me callous. But the cruelty of the camp made me see reality in an unexpected light. Those who accepted the truth did not make it through. They gave up every hope and perished. I clung to the hope that I would survive. I believed it. I steeled myself against emotional traps. I did my best to escape the reality. I noticed this in many others, too.

The days at the Omarska camp were always unpredictable. It was never possible to tell with any certainty what was going to happen in the next two minutes. There was constant tension in the air. The Chetniks started beating us just for two cigarettes. They wanted watches, shoes, trainers, gold.

Seiko watches and Adidas shoes and trainers were the brands they were after. Some inmates had expensive Swiss watches, each of which was worth several kilos of Seikos, but no: 'Fuck that rubbish,' they would say, 'we want Seikos.' As the weeks passed, every Chetnik was rolling up his sleeve proudly displaying 'his' Seiko.

On our way to the canteen, the guards would be 'scanning' our shoes. They would take those with *Alpinke* (a popular name in Bosnia for Adidas mountain boots) out of the queue. In exchange for giving up their *Alpinke* 'voluntarily', they would be given a pair of shoes taken from those who had died on previous nights. At first, the dead had been taken away with their shoes on. When the craze for *Alpinke* started, hundreds of pairs of shoes taken from the dead were piled up next to the staircase leading to my floor.

When all the Adidas shoes were gone, the Chetniks started showing interest in Adidas trainers. I guess they wanted to have a pair of each. Kasim was again unlucky here. He wore brand new trainers. While we were queuing for a meal, Drazenko Predojevic approached him and asked: 'What size are they?'

'Forty one.'

'Just my size,' he declared. As one of the Serbian songs says — 'Take everything that life offers you...'

On the way back, Kasim was taken aside by Drazenko while the rest of us went straight back to the room. Two minutes later, Kasim walked in barefoot. He was not even offered replacement shoes. I was not surprised as Drazenko picked on him all the time. Others wearing Adidas trainers realised what was in store for them. Maruf and Ibro cut pieces out of their trainers and so saved them from confiscation.

Other guards preferred to take our possessions when nobody could see their faces. They would enter our room after midnight, ordering us to lie down facing the floor with our hands clasped behind our heads. The light would go on and they would walk around picking out shoes, leather jackets, and trainers. We never wore any footwear inside our rooms — we were trying to create some illusion of hygiene. Zahid, who slept inside the shower cubicle next to mine, advised me several times to damage my trainers.

'They look too good,' he said. 'Sooner or later they will take them away.'

I was not worried that much. My trainers were a less well-known brand, and they had unattractive colours.

11

Time went slowly. Each new day in the camp brought its share of surprises — but still, in a morbid way, every day was the same. People would be taken out of the room. Some came back walking; others needed support; still others never came back. They ended up on the yellow lorry. People were taken out, at all times, during the day and night, without explanation. Even though the whole operation which had brought us to Omarska was masterminded from above, there were no organised procedures by which the guards and the camp authorities were guided. There were no timetables — even for the killings. They just went on round the clock. And those doing the killing were clearly following the instructions of their superiors. For some, there was the additional 'pleasure' of resolving old disputes between neighbours, colleagues, students and teachers. Death became a way of life. I became numb. Fear was the only feeling I had left, and I was steeped in it. I sat there thinking, 'Will I be next? Will they come for me?' The same question was visible in everybody's eyes. What will happen to me? Where's my family? What's happened to them?

Zahid had two daughters and a son. With the setting sun, Zahid would sigh: 'Where are you now, son?'

Half of the original number of us held in Room 24 had 'disappeared'. Day after day, there was more space on the floor. Just when I got the chance to stretch out fully on the floor, the guards ordered all of us to move to Room 15, on the other side of the corridor. Room 15 was chock-a-block. The first few to enter the room found some space, but the rest of us were left standing.

Room 15 had three different sections. In the section next to the door, there were some two hundred people almost on top of each other. A further two hundred men were squeezed into another similar section at the far end. There were no windows. The middle section had previously been used by miners for washing after work. Half of it contained sinks and half of it showers. The shower section had one small window high up on the wall. A narrow passage ran between the shower room and the sink room, connecting the front and back sections of the room. There were ten showers — five on each side. The whole shower section measured less than twenty square metres.

This Thursday evening, when we were brought into Room 15, most of the people in the shower section were from my village. But everybody said: 'Look somewhere else. There isn't enough space in here.' Any feeling of empathy — the very feeling that makes humans different from other animals — had gone. We had become like animals. Everyone defended his own territory. Newcomers became unwanted intruders. A battle for survival was going on. There really was not enough room for all of us to sit down — and yet a bit of space could still have been made to squeeze in Kasim and myself. After all, we had been neighbours all our lives. I was bitter. I felt like shouting: 'You dirty, selfish bastards! Don't you know where you are?'

But I suppressed the impulse, realising that my anger would be to no avail. And then, to our surprise, we were invited to sit down by a man we did not know. The shower cubicles at that time stood empty, as before our arrival it had been forbidden to use the shower section as accommodation. So we settled in one of the cubicles. Apart from the fact that we were two men occupying less than one square metre, it was a stroke of luck because we could not easily be spotted when the guards opened the door at night. Also, it was near the only window — so we got some fresh air occasionally. Those still standing and looking for a space to sit down created a noise which enraged the Chetniks. They came in and shouted: 'Shut up and sit down!'

All of a sudden, somehow, everybody sat down.

The occupants of the shower section came from all walks of life — labourers, bus drivers, technicians, judges, computer experts, right down to the technical director of this very mine.

From the moment I settled in the showers, and for the next six days, I watched a man dying. His name was Miro Solaja. He was a Croat. He was a big, strong man in his late fifties or early sixties. Now, the upper part of his body was black and blue. He had been badly beaten. He was in agony. He was feverish and seemed unaware of his surroundings, even though his eyes were wide open. The night before, the Chetniks had taken him out, tied him to a lamp-post and beaten him with the handles of shovels. His right arm was broken. To ease his pain, Stjepan 'Stipe' Maric daily massaged his back and the broken arm. He put compresses on him, and even made some support for his arm out of carton boxes. But day after day, Solaja's condition was worsening. He could no longer breathe properly. The sounds coming from his throat were more like a death rattle. I thought he might suffocate, for he could no longer inhale enough air. He could not go to the canteen. It was usually Husein, the trader, who brought food to him. Stipe put small pieces of bread in Solaja's soup, and fed him like a baby. Eventually, a sickening smell started to emanate from Solaja. He was rotting inside — it was the smell of death. He was taken to the room for the sick, and the following morning the Chetniks came to the door asking for four strong men. Solaja was dead. They carried him outside the building.

A few days before Solaja's death, a Chetnik from Prijedor came to see him. Solaja's wife, Mira, had asked him to check how Solaja was doing. He could not give the message to Solaja — who was hardly conscious — but looking around, he suddenly asked Omer Kerenovic, a judge from Prijedor: 'Do you remember the time you fined me for a traffic offence?'

'It was my job as a judge,' Omer replied. Suddenly, enraged, the Chetnik cursed him and then left — growling threats.

Omer explained to us that the offence had happened in the late 1970s. Obviously, in the Chetnik's eyes it was not a punishment given by a judge to an offender, but a punishment by a Muslim inflicted on a Serb, just because he was a Serb. A few days later, Omer was transferred from the showers to the garage in the administration building. There he was killed.

I still hoped and believed I would live to see the end of this suffering. Even though at times I fell prey to depression, I refused to believe that bullets or truncheons would end my life. I felt determined to endure all the waiting. But willpower could not feed my body. I was getting weaker every day. My daily diet was fear, for both Kasim and myself. From time to time, I would try to escape from it by talking our situation over with those around me. But it would turn out that these monotonous discussions of what, when, if, and how, raised questions and speculations which led back to the fear from which I was trying to escape.

Another way to get away from this madhouse was to spend some minutes each day in psychological solitude, thinking about

Mama. I still did not know where she was or how she was, but I wanted to think and hope that she was well and safe. Day after day in my thoughts, I sent good wishes to her. Then, one day, a 'messenger' arrived. It was Sead Sivac, our cousin from Trnopolje. Neither Kasim nor I knew he was in Omarska. The first thing he told us was that Mama was alive and well. This was a huge relief. We then listened to his story about his journey from Trnopolje to Omarska. At first he had been taken to Keraterm, where he was labelled as one of those involved in preparations for defence, and he almost died as a result of beatings. Then he was transferred to Omarska. He was on his way to recovery.

Some stray cows with huge and swollen udders appeared at the camp, mooing as if to ask us to help them get rid of the huge burden of milk they carried and to relieve their pain. Once, when we were sitting on the grass after the meal, waiting to be ordered back inside, some men asked the guards whether they could milk them. Sead was one of those who asked. It seemed an opportunity to get some milk. The guards reacted angrily and said: 'You don't know how to milk a cow.' But Sead replied, 'I'm a vet.' So the Chetniks let him milk a cow that stood on the 'pista'.

Now, Sead sometimes even had a cheerful smile on his face. He seemed to think that the worst was over. His wounds from Keraterm had healed. But then he was taken out and beaten again. His back was black. However, he began to recover for a second time. His zest for life was still there. I spoke to him for the last time when we were given a 'bath' with a hose pipe.

'How's it going?' I joined him in picking some green blackberries which grew in the space close to the 'Red House' where we were hosed down.

'All right,' he said, smiling at me.

'You don't want to have a "bath" either?'

'No.' He kept smiling.

Soon after, he was taken out and murdered in the middle of

the day.

We learnt this from S. H., Sead's neighbour, who on the day Sead was killed was walking from the canteen back to the 'White House' when he was asked by a guard: 'Why are you barefoot? Where are your shoes?'

'I lost them somewhere around,' he lied.

The truth was that for several consecutive nights, S. H. had been beaten in the 'White House' together with a group of over twenty other inmates. The bloody trail of each night's beatings led to the grass behind the building. As a result of these beatings, S. H. had lost his shoes. He did not even remember exactly when this had happened. He had lost track of time. All he thought about was survival. Walking around barefoot was irrelevant.

'Come with me,' the guard said. They went behind the 'White House'. 'I feel sorry for you,' the guard said. 'You're so young.'

Hearing these words and looking at dead bodies lying on the grass, S. H. thought his last moment had come.

'Do you know any of these men?' The guard pointed to the bodies.

'No, I don't.'

'Are you sure?'

'Yes.'

S. H. lied. He recognised not one, but several of the bodies. Some of them had been beaten along with him the previous night. He did not recognise their faces. They no longer had any faces. He recognised the overalls and shoes of Hune, his friend and neighbour. He also recognised Sead's shirt and trousers.

'Choose a pair,' the guard said. S. H. took the shoes from the dead body of his friend Hune.

People in the camp could be divided into those who believed in life, those who had given up life, and those who after weeks of incarceration still had not come to terms with what had happened to them. For this last group, the world of Omarska was not real. There were also those who wanted to live, but who knew that survival was unlikely. They knew they would not leave Omarska alive. I never knew whether it was intuition or some new sense they had developed in the camp over time.

Sead had been a believer and a fighter. Every time they beat him, he had fought very hard to recover from his physical and psychological wounds. But when he was taken out for the last time, the guards had given him no more opportunities.

Miroslav 'Buco' was a fighter, too. Buco, a Croat and a former employee of the mine, came to the window by our corner to get a breath of fresh air. Before I got to know him, he had kept himself to himself, quietly spending his days in the section with the sinks. Then the guards took him out. When they brought him back, even the shirt on his back had been torn to shreds by heavy blows. They had started by beating his palms with a truncheon. He had shown no sign of pain or emotion and this had infuriated the guards. They wanted to humiliate him. They wanted him to cry out. They beat him savagely, but Buco did not oblige. They never heard him cry for mercy.

After this beating, he started coming to the window. He needed to escape from the stench of the excrement floating in the sink. From time to time, he would join in a game of cards. I got to know him quite well.

He had ended up in the camp for spitting on the obituary poster of a Serb officer. He was reported to the police and brought to Omarska. He was an ordinary bloke — interested in books and sports. His favourite book was *Shogun*, by James Clavell. He spoke to me about this book often. I had seen the screen adaptation, but he said that the spirit of the book and its characters could never be fully presented in pictures: 'To understand it you have to take the time to read the book.'

He had been an active wrestler, and his physique was still

incredible. He was strong, but also very gentle. For a man of his bulk, he walked lightly and his voice was quiet and soft. His back was beginning to get better. When it seemed he was on his way to recovery, the Chetniks took him out for the last time. One of them started hitting him even before they closed the door, and the other one said, 'Don't beat him. He's an employee of the mine.'

The next day, his body was seen by a man whose task was to load dead bodies on to the yellow lorry. The Chetniks had gouged out his eyes. Our conversations were finished for ever.

Months later, when I was a free man in the Red Cross Reception Centre in Karlovac, a man came into the room inquiring about his brother. He showed us his photograph. It was Buco. I told him that Buco had been with us in Omarska, but I had no heart to tell him that he was dead, as I would have had to tell him the way in which he had died. I simply could not.

Dido was one of those who knew they would not leave the camp alive. Unlike Sead and Buco, he had faced the truth. He was kept in the small room in the garage. One day, he appeared in the showers. He had managed to come and see us for a short visit.

'Folks,' he said, 'I'm melting. Every day, more and more of my body is disappearing.' But this was not what worried him most. 'Each day, I wait to be taken out,' he said. He did not look frightened, but rather seemed to be prepared. This visit turned out to be his last goodbye to us.

Terrible things that Dido had heard about from the guards were still unknown to us then — and he did not talk to us about these things during his visit. Those staying with him in the garage told me later that Dido had been asked by the Chetniks whether he would be willing to go to Banja Luka and join a Serb girl, Bilja, who was from Omarska and with whom he had had a son. Bilja was a shop assistant who had worked for a time in the grocery shop in my village. During that time, she and Dido had developed a relationship. They never married, but Bilja had given birth to a son. They had never lived together, and when the relationship eventually ended, Bilja kept the boy.

Now in Omarska, some years later, Dido was told that Bilja was working at the airport in Banja Luka and was willing to take him back. However, Dido knew that if he went to Banja Luka he would have to join the Serb army. He declined this offer and decided to stay in the camp. Soon after he left us, Dido's worst fears had come true. Zeljko Meakic took him out. The beating started immediately in the garage.

We were told later by a family who lived in the village of Omarska at that time that they had seen him being dragged along a street, surrounded by a great number of the locals. He was all torn and bloody and everybody was trying to get a punch or a kick into him. He never came back. He was never heard of again. Zeljko Meakic, who had taken him out, would know exactly where and how his life ended.

Dido was a wonderful guy. I had known him my whole life and everybody loved him. He had never harmed a single person and was great fun to be with. His disappearance is a great loss for all of us, but our memory of him will never die.

12

The first people to be interrogated were 'extremists' and 'fighters' — then those named by others under torture. After that, selection was random. They would come to the room and point at several people without rhyme or reason. Finally, they would come into the room and say: 'Who wants to be interrogated next?'

By this time we had realised that sooner or later everyone would be interrogated — so those who wanted to get it over and done with would get up and volunteer. Most people were thinking: 'I didn't commit any crime. I'm just a civilian and have nothing to hide. The sooner I get it over with the better.'

Kasim and I knew our turn would come, but we were of the opinion that it was better to wait for these volunteers to go first. There was no need to rush. There were people who believed that once everybody had been interrogated they would let us go.

Often those interrogated were given 'confessions' to sign

without being allowed to read them. Some of those who signed died, while others were never touched afterwards. Two men from my village, who had been interrogated several times, signed such 'confessions' — and yet they survived.

Being called out again after the first interrogation almost certainly meant execution. Suad Foric had decided to keep quiet when the guards came to take him out — calling him by his name and his father's name. He was lucky that almost nobody knew his father's real name, for his father had been better known under a different name. Usually on such occasions, other inmates would indicate to the guards that such and such a person was in the room by stupidly shouting: 'Hey, So-and-so, the guards are looking for you.' This made it impossible for anybody to hide. But Suad had managed it thanks to his father's being better known by his nickname.

Kasim always expected the guards would one day come and take him out. He never told me much about his fears, but I knew it was there deep down inside him.

When the Chetnik attack on our village was imminent, Kasim and some other people had bought rifles for themselves from Serbian black-marketeers. Kasim surrendered this rifle the day after the attack, but in the camp it was the sword of Damocles which hung above his head. It was also his shadow. The more guards that knew about it, the more dangerous this fact became.

During one meal, Drazenko Predojevic was asking everyone: 'Is there somebody from Kevljani called Haco in this group?' Many groups passed through the canteen and nobody said anything — even though many knew who Drazenko was looking for. But there is always someone prepared to speak without compulsion.

'It isn't Haco, but Kace,' Sejo said, and he gave Drazenko Kasim's full name. When Kasim and I entered the canteen, Drazenko had already discovered the full name. Fearing that somebody else in the group might point at him, Kasim said: 'It's me.'

'Where's your pistol? Where did you hide it?' Kasim also had a legally-owned pistol. Drazenko, one of the most notorious camp guards, was very drunk, and it was anybody's guess whether he was more dangerous when he was sober or when he was under the influence.

'I didn't hide it. I surrendered it,' Kasim replied.

'Serif's daughter-in-law, Gordana, found your pistol buried beneath a window of your house.'

'She could find nothing there. I surrendered my pistol,' Kasim repeated again.

While this went on, Kasim started eating. He realised that time was passing, and he would have to leave his meal on the table. When he finished the soup, he passed his piece of bread to me saying: 'Put it inside your jumper. They're going to beat me up now.' I did as he told me.

Drazenko waited in the corridor. Kasim was behind me. Drazenko tried to trip me, but I jumped over his foot and Kasim did the same. We ran fast across the tarmac area. Drazenko was too drunk to follow.

A few times, Kasim had mentioned he was even thinking of making an attempt to escape out the window and over the roof using the rain as cover. He had thought it all out very carefully, but I was his biggest concern. Had he succeeded, he was afraid I would have to pay the price.

When it became possible to count the number of inmates from Room 15 who had not yet been questioned, we decided to face our interrogators. But this — as always — did not depend on us. Everything depended on what the guards and the camp administrators would decide to do.

One day, an escort soldier came to our room and called out Kasim's name. My whole world collapsed. Days before, several guys from my village were confirming to the interrogators that Kasim had possessed arms. During one of those breaks we had on the grass after the meal, Siljo said to me: 'Tell Kasim that I confessed to the interrogators that I was using his Kalashnikov during the time when we organised village patrols.'

I could not believe my ears. I never thought he would try to hide himself behind Kasim. He was putting Kasim's life at risk in order to save his own skin. He had buried his own pistol — the one Kasim had got for him when he wanted a weapon. I was furious. And now, Kasim was called out.

'Is this it?' I thought. 'Is he coming back?'

Most of those called out before him did not return. Those that did were badly beaten, and always expecting to be called out again. Kasim always feared that this would happen. More than anything else in the world, I wanted him to come back.

Seconds and minutes became like eternity. I felt so lonely. When he left, I felt a part of me had left, too. I waited. Then the door opened and he came in. My prayers had been answered. He was badly beaten, but still on his feet. The only thing that mattered was that he was still alive.

As a dozen people had already told the interrogators that Kasim had had a Kalashnikov, he could not deny it so he had confessed to owning the weapon. The beating he had received had been interspersed with questions. Miroslav Zoric, one of the interrogators, had asked: 'Do you know Emir Karabasic?' Emir was our neighbour and my former classmate — he had been interrogated some thirty minutes before Kasim had been called out.

'Yes, I do.'

'So, do you want us to bring Emir in here?' Clearly, Emir had connected Kasim with something else. Kasim did not let Zoric frighten him with this threat.

'You can bring whoever you want to. I know I didn't do

anything wrong.'

Zoric and the other interrogator — dressed in civilian clothes — decided that Kasim needed further softening to make him more co-operative. The guard who had brought Kasim to the room was very young — probably in his twenties, and physically fit. He enjoyed beating. He punched Kasim, slapping him on both ears with open palms. This sent Kasim through noisy tunnels of pain and darkness. He still had some strength to remain seated on the chair. Falling on the floor meant being kicked to death. He kept his head very low — trying to protect his face and chest. The guard grabbed a long piece of wood and kept hitting him with it over the back until the wood broke. Then, it was time for the blows to the head with a police truncheon — followed by kicks in the rib cage.

Kasim believed that if he 'confessed' to what they wanted, they would kill him. If he persisted in protesting his innocence (and he *was* innocent), maybe they would give up.

For many days afterwards, Kasim coughed up blood. The kicks had left almost no marks, but the pain in his chest was unbearable. We suspected some of his ribs might have been broken.

Some people had volunteered information to the interrogators that they had never been asked to provide. They must have thought: 'If I tell them everything I know, everything I heard, even if I didn't see it for myself, they won't beat me.'

If they had kept their mouths shut, more lives would have been saved. Others, like Kahro, had kept to themselves things they knew about for sure — even at the price of heavy beatings. They beat the hell out of him, but he kept on saying: 'I know nothing. You can kill me, but I know nothing.'

The day after Kasim's interrogation, it was my turn. I did not know what to expect. All those who went before me had had different experiences. Some had been killed; some severely beaten.

Some had been forced to their knees to say Muslim prayers — even though most of us were not religious and did not even know how to pray. Some did not receive even a single blow. It all seemed to depend on who the interrogators were, and what mood they were in on that particular day. It was a lottery.

Ten of us were escorted towards the administration building. At the entrance, they told us: 'Wait here. When you see another prisoner coming back from the interrogation, one of you go upstairs. There you'll be directed to one of the rooms.'

The wooden bench used by the guards as a hurdle on our way to the canteen was unoccupied. No guard stood nearby, so several of us sat on it. They did not have to keep an eye on us. We could not go anywhere else but inside the building. The first inmate came down the stairs. He ran manically towards the seated crowd on the 'pista'. I was soon to discover why he had been running so fast.

I let some five or six men go upstairs before me. I was trying not to think about anything other than to concentrate on what was ahead of me. While I was waiting, men kept running out of the building at full speed.

Finally, I entered the building myself, went upstairs, and stopped on the top of the staircase. A long corridor with several offices on each side stretched before me. Not knowing where to go, I waited for the two guards who were there to tell me what to do next. I recognised them both. The one with the long beard and moustache had a nickname, 'Baba'. The other one was the one who had beaten up Kasim the day before.

'Go to the last door on your left,' the latter said. As I was going down the corridor, he yelled behind me: 'Not so slow! Faster, faster! Run!'

I knocked on the door and waited.

'What are you waiting for? Get in there,' he yelled again.

I opened the door. It was a big room. There was a long table running the length of the opposite wall. Behind it, right in front of me, was a civilian interrogator with his nose deep in a pile of papers. On his left, there was a mattress placed vertically across the table, dividing it into two separate parts.

'Good afternoon,' I said. He raised his head and said: 'Over there.' He nodded towards two men on his left behind the mattress.

I went there and was told to sit down in the chair opposite them. They were the same interrogators Kasim had seen the day before. The civilian one sat at the table. He was immaculate. Dark hair carefully combed. Moustache carefully trimmed. Spotlessly clean white shirt with short sleeves.

The other interrogator was Miroslav Zoric, a tall man in his late thirties. He was standing and was dressed in military fatigues. At Electrotechnical School in Prijedor, he had been one of my teachers for one semester. He did not recognise me. He liked to joke.

For a minute or two, they just scrutinised me. They said nothing, they asked nothing, they just stared at me as if I were some kind of a very rare species they rarely came across. I returned their gaze — deeming it wise not to drop my eyes, as this might be interpreted as a sign of an uneasy conscience. They were also interested in my long hair tied in a bun.

'Are you a male or a female?' Zoric finally broke the silence, laughing.

'Male,' I replied in a matter-of-fact way.

'What's your name?' his colleague asked.

'Kemal Pervanic.'

'Do you have any document to prove it?'

'I have an ID card.'

'Let me see it.' I pulled it from the back pocket of my jeans and handed it over the table.

'What's your relation to Sakib Pervanic?' he asked while

preparing the list of names. Sakib's name was just ahead of mine on the list. I realised that Sakib had been interrogated this same afternoon by these two.

'He's my neighbour.'

'Just neighbour or maybe a cousin?'

'Just a neighbour.' They had another long, close look at me. I seemed to have developed a sixth sense. It was telling me that the best defence strategy was to give short answers. This way, I would avoid the trap of making unnecessary statements.

'What's your occupation?'

'Electronics technician.'

'Where did you do your course?'

'In Prijedor.'

I looked at Zoric, expecting him to react to this. But he did not.

Zoric was not the only teacher from my school days in Prijedor who was present each day in the camp. Nada Balaban, who had been my English teacher for four years, was here, too. My teachers of yesterday were my judges today. Back then they had decided what grades I should get — now they were deciding whether I should live or die.

'Are you married?'

'No, I'm not.'

'Who else have you got in your family?'

'Parents and two brothers.'

'Where's your father and what is his occupation?'

'He's in Zagreb, working for a telecommunications company.'

'And your mother?'

'She's a housewife.'

'Where are your brothers?'

'One is here with me, and the elder one is in Zagreb working for a construction company.'

At this point, Zoric took over. He fired a barrage of questions at me. The reason for this attack was that my father and my brother both worked in Croatia.

'Didn't your father bring you a nice machine gun from Croatia?'

'No, he didn't.'

'Is your brother a Zenga?'[3]

'No, he isn't. He spent the whole winter at home. He went back to work in late March.'

'We have information that the Croatian Army had recruited many new Zengas in March. Many of them Muslims.'

'But not my brother.' I tried to keep my answers firm and short.

'Did you do your National Service?'

'Yes.'

'Where and when?'

'In Brcko, from January 1988 to January 1989.'

'Why didn't you then join our army to fight the *Ustashe*?'

'I didn't want to join any army in this conflict. I didn't join Alija (Izetbegovic), so I didn't join you either.'

'Did you sign up to join the Bosnian Army?' He ignored my previous answer.

I knew they had a list with the names of all the guys from my village who had done their National Service. Kasim had told me about it the day before. Apart from the names, the list also stated the type of training we had been given during the Service. There had been no Bosnian Army at this time. At one point, somebody had had the bright idea to 'conscript' for the 'Bosnian Army'. They

---

3. When a new government was elected in Croatia in 1990, its police force tried to establish its authority in Knin, a part of Croatia predominantly populated by the Croatian Serbs. The locals did not allow the new police force into the town. The JNA threatened the Croatian government. At that time, Croatia had no armed force to protect herself. The ruling party, the Croatian Democratic Union (HDZ), started to arm its members. The name of this new force was Zbor Narodne Garde (ZNG). Its members were popularly called Zenge (Zenge plural; Zenga singular) — a name derived from the abbreviation (Ze eN Ga). When Croatia became recognised as an independent state, the Croatian Army (HV) was formed, with Zenge making up its core. The Serbs kept calling HV members Zenge.

went with a piece of paper from house to house, asking whether we wanted to 'join'. The only weapon this 'army' had had was this idea of registration. All the 'soldiers' continued to live at home, going about their daily chores. At the time of the attack, somebody had remembered to burn this list — otherwise we would all have perished. The Serbs had got wind of this list, but they never got the names on it because it had been burnt.

'No, I didn't.' I felt safe denying their claim as I knew they did not have the list.

'You're lying.'

'No, I'm not.'

'Yes, you are.'

'No, I'm not.'

'Don't make me go and fetch the list.'

'I signed nothing.'

Zoric left the room. Minutes later, he was back with a list.

'What did you say your name was?' he asked again. 'Why are you lying? Here is your name on the list.' The list he brought had no signatures, and all the names on it were in the same handwriting.

'I heard that somebody from my village made a list of all men who did National Service. This must be it. Somebody must have given my details.' I stuck to my story.

'What were you trained for during your Service?'

'I was trained how to fire rockets.'

'In other words, you planned to shell the Serbs.' This was obvious sarcasm and I made no reply.

At this point, Zoran Delic came in with coffee.

'Because you haven't been honest with us, take your chair and sit in that corner.' The civilian interrogator pointed to the corner behind me. 'Sit there while we're having coffee.'

Sitting in the corner, I tried to remain calm. I tried to be prepared for whatever would come next.

During the break, other Chetniks came into the room. An older man with fair hair and a moustache, dressed like Zoric, looked at me and asked: 'Who's that? Are you a woman or a gay?' He laughed. I did not say anything.

'He's meditating,' he said, laughing again and leaving the room. Then the young guard who yelled at me in the corridor came in. He stood behind me saying angrily: 'You Turkish motherfucker, if it weren't for you, I would not be here today. I would now be peacefully at home.' He was saying this with complete conviction — as if we were the ones who had wanted trouble and started the killings. I saw him raise his right arm, and I closed my eyes. He struck me with his elbow on the back. Nothing else followed and I opened my eyes. I was lucky. He did not seem to have the time to beat me. He was afraid they would drink up all the coffee without him.

On the small windowsill next to me, there was a pair of scissors. I was suddenly terrified that he might stab me with them. What were those scissors doing there? What were they for?

They were having their coffee and paying no attention to me. Luck seemed to be on my side. One blow was insignificant compared to what others had endured. But I remained apprehensive about the scissors, and about the presence of this particular Chetnik. I could not predict what he was going to do next.

After the coffee break, their faces looked happier. Coffee seemed to have softened them up a bit. It was already late in the afternoon. 'It'll soon be time for them to go home,' I hoped.

They resumed the interrogation.

'What do you know about preparations for organised defence against the Serbian Army?'

'Nothing. I don't know about any such activities. All I know is that we had patrols in the village during the night.'

'Who were you afraid of? *Ustashe*? Chetniks? Rabbits?' Zoric interrupted. His questions were pompous and absurd — but I chose to answer him in all seriousness, no matter how ridiculous his queries.

'At first, the patrols had been mixed — Serbs and Muslims. Later on, we were told by neighbour-Serbs to guard our village ourselves, and they would guard theirs. We weren't told why we should keep watch. That's all I know.'

'Who possessed arms in your village?'

'I don't know. I didn't see any weapons. I know only that several men were given M48s some weeks earlier by the Territorial Defence in Prijedor. Whether anybody else bought a rifle for himself, I would not be able to tell you. An organised distribution of arms never took place.'

Actually, those who had Kalashnikovs had bought them on the black market from Serbian soldiers. Any kind of weapon had been available provided you had enough money. Kasim once told me: 'I could have bought an anti-tank gun and a mine-thrower if I had had the money.'

'You're joking!'

'I'm serious. An officer at the barracks offered it to me. I asked, "How am I to smuggle an anti-tank gun out?" He said, 'Just bring a lorry and five thousand German marks and park the lorry at the gates. The gun has wheels. I'll pull it out and we'll load it on the lorry. No problem."'

'Where were you during the attack?' The interrogation carried on.

'At home.'

'Did your village give any resistance?'

'No. The whole village spent the night of the attack in the river bed. Next morning, we surrendered to the local army commander without firing a single shot.'

At this point, they both got tired of me. Zoric said to his colleague: 'He's not the one.' Whether he meant that I was not an extremist or a Muslim fundamentalist, or something else, I could not tell. The civilian interrogator then scribbled something at the bottom of his notes and said: 'You can go now.' As I was leaving, he said, 'Wait. You left your ID card.' I had known that. I preferred to skip asking whether I could take it back. I could not predict their response.

On the way back, I realised why everybody had been sprinting out of the building. The guards at the top of the stairs were hitting people passing between them at random. Speed was essential. Running down the corridor, I saw 'Baba' stretch his right leg out across the first step. I knew if I had to jump over it, he would lift his leg and trip me.

'If I fall down the stairs, I might break a leg,' I thought.

I slowed down — looking at Baba's eyes. He withdrew his leg. The other one barked: 'Faster, faster.'

I ran down the stairs like thunder. At the bottom of the stairs, there was another bastard delivering additional blows. I ran so fast that he did not even make an attempt to hit me. I had not known myself that I could run that fast. I stormed straight out into the crowd on the 'pista'. They were all stretched out on the ground lying face-down. I ran between their bodies, trying to get closer to the wall. Those on the edge were exposed to the guards and their blows.

I lay there in the scorching sun for forty minutes at least. Sweat was pouring down my face. When the guards gave us a signal to get up, I was sent to Room 24.

The next day, I managed to sneak back to my room. My old place in the shower already had another occupant. I had to find a new place. There was a place in a shower cubicle just opposite.

'Is anybody staying in here?' I asked my neighbours.

'Hodza's son stays in there now,' Zahid said to me.

The cubicle was empty and I went to see Hodza Sakib, to ask whether his son still wanted to keep the place.

'No. I found him some space here. He's going to stay with

me,' Hodza kindly replied. My luck had served me once more.

By camp 'standards', my interrogation had gone well — but I could not stop worrying about my long hair attracting the guards' attention. Twice, Drazenko Predojevic stopped me on the way to the canteen. Both times, he ordered me to cut my hair off, and to report to him the following day. The third time, he said: 'Why didn't you cut your hair as I told you?'

'I have nothing to cut it with.'

'You have another twenty-four hours to do it.' This time, I had to find some way to cut it.

I went to another part of the room to ask Bahrija to lend me his scissors. People around me told me that he and his nephews had cut their hair. They went to the toilet and had a haircut while Husein kept watch. Now in silence, they all looked at each other and Bahrija said: 'I don't have scissors.'

Explaining to them why I had to have it done, I said that Senad would cut my hair in my shower cubicle and nobody would see the scissors. But Bahrija was too frightened. I understood his caution and went back to my place.

When Said, another neighbour staying in the showers, heard about my problem, he managed to get a razor from somewhere.

'How would you like it?' he asked me seriously.

'Just cut it off,' I said to him.

'No, no,' he said, 'if we are going to do it, we'll do it the best way we can.'

'Said, there is no need for hair-styling.'

'Yes, there is.'

I was anxious to have my hair cut short and I couldn't care less about the way I looked afterwards. But for Said, this act of cutting my hair was not merely about reducing its length. For him, giving me a nice haircut meant maintaining some humanity — keeping some dignity. In these moments of my humiliation, he wanted me to look nice when facing Drazenko and all the others who ill-treated me because of my long hair. For his part, he wanted to do a good job of which he could be proud. He cut it in a most professional way.

'I owe you for this.'

'You owe me nothing,' he said absent-mindedly, engrossed in his work.

'I'll get you a bottle of cognac once we are free.'

'OK,' he smiled.

13

We also experienced a miracle. Sakib had smuggled a portable radio into the camp. We could receive news from three major stations — Radio Sarajevo, Radio Zagreb, and Radio Belgrade. Information given to us by the guards could not be trusted, and we tried to form our own opinion about the overall situation in Bosnia based on radio news. We listened to the late evening news, because then we were less likely to be caught by the guards — and the signals were clearer at night.

Among the first news we heard was that the UN Security Council had passed a resolution imposing economic sanctions on rump Yugoslavia — that is, its 'constituent' members Serbia and Montenegro. This gave us some hope. If Serbia did not stop this aggression, then the international community would not let the Serbs wipe out the whole of the Bosnian Muslim population. We all waited for the moment when the Serbs would face reprisals by the Western powers — those who had so readily expelled Saddam

Hussein from Kuwait just a year ago.

But time passed, and nothing happened. Comments started to circulate such as: 'We don't have any oil, and Bosnia isn't strategically important,' and: 'In Kuwait the Allied forces were killing Muslims; to send troops to Bosnia would mean killing Christians.'

These opinions were triggered by despair. Hopes were fading, and help was not forthcoming. No one seemed to be willing to come to our rescue.

Some lucky inmates got transferred to Trnopolje and then to Central Bosnia — from where some who had relatives in Croatia could go there. During one of the news broadcasts we received in those days, we heard that some of these men had told of the existence of Omarska and the other camps in the area to the Croatian media. They were the people who had suffered along with us. They knew of our plight, and we thought: 'Now the world knows for sure what's going on here — it can't last much longer.' But it did. It lasted too long for some. The question that will haunt me for the rest of my life is: 'Did the world *want to know*?'

After the news of the visit of the French President, François Mitterrand, to Sarajevo, everybody lost the last shreds of hope that the Serbs would be punished. We all saw clearly that there would be no military intervention.

The only remaining hope was that the Bosnian Government might exchange us for the soldiers from Bosanski Brod held by the Bosnian Muslim–Croat forces. The guards said that such an initiative had been made on the Serbian side, but that our side was refusing to enter into any such agreement. Listening to the news night after night, we realised that no exchange in which we would be involved was ever going to take place. Some started to believe that we had been sacrificed by the Bosnian Government for the purpose of triggering an international response. Bitter disappointment was becoming ever more bitter. Some persistently asked the guards: 'When are we going to be released?' And the standard answer was: 'You'll go home very soon. We need to capture several groups of extremists in the Kozara Mountain who are still refusing to surrender, and then you'll go home.'

This was strongly contradicted by people who were for one reason or another taken by the guards back to our villages. Kevac, a middle-aged man from my village, had been taken back to his home by the Serb police to find the documents of registration and ownership for his lorry. He had passed through the whole village, as his house stood at its far end. Lorries and tractor trailers were standing in front of the houses, loaded with plundered goods.

Throughout the last six or seven years, my village had been going through a period of great transformation. Many new houses had been built, and many more were in the process of construction. The Chetniks were taking everything: building materials such as bricks, roof tiles, and timber; technical goods such as electric cookers, fridges, TV and VCR sets; household items; everything. Our Serb neighbours competed with some privately funded armed groups committed to organised looting. Their local sponsor was Milan Andjic, who had a warehouse in Prijedor where clothing, footwear, technical goods and other pillaged items were being carefully sorted out. From Prijedor, these goods were transported to Belgrade, where Andjic had another warehouse. From there, it was all sold to people in Serbia. This made the army leaders and people like Milan Andjic millionaires. We later heard that the looters would occasionally shoot each other over their 'claims' to a particular house.

On his trip, Kevac noticed that naked walls were all that remained of some of the houses. Window frames, whole roofs and doors had been taken out. Cables, sockets and everything else that could be removed from the walls was gone. Other houses, with all their contents, had been burnt to the ground as an act of personal revenge. The camp leaders, Zeljko Meakic and Miroslav Kvocka, regularly came to the camp in a Mercedes car formerly owned by Dijaz Hadzic, one of my neighbours. Zeljko had known this man all his life, and had simply demanded the keys and the registration papers in order to take possession of the car — all in the 'service' of his people.

Weeks after the first wave of plunder, the whole village had been destroyed. Some camp guards liked to tell us about the destruction they had seen and in which they had sometimes personally taken part. They enjoyed telling us anything that would, if possible, cause us even greater misery. Hasim and his younger brother, Halid, had played football for F. C. Omarska for years. In this way, they had made a lot of Serb friends — some of whom now acted as guards. One of the guards told them that he had been in our village in search of hidden valuables. Walking down the road, he had spotted some things scattered across a garden. His curiosity had taken him into the garden and among other things he had seen a family album. In the album, he had recognised Hasim and Halid in some of the pictures. Hasim and Halid had buried this family album, together with some other things in the garden. So it really was true that the Serbs were ploughing gardens in search of valuables. Huse, an old villager, had made a joke about Serbian treasure hunters. 'A shell landed in my garden,' he said, 'and dug out all Nafa's gold.' Nafa was his wife.

Another guard, Emsud's former schoolmate, described Emsud's house to him. Most of the things from the house had been looted. Windows had been broken and beneath them lay the scattered remains of furniture. His guess was that as those who had looted Emsud's house probably could not take it all with them — they had destroyed what was left rather than leave anything behind. Leaving the house, he had set it on fire. He wanted Emsud to know that it was he himself who had burnt it down.

Even after such stories, and despite the smoke which we could see rising above our villages, some guys still hoped that one day we would go home again. But home was no more.

One particular piece of radio news made everybody in the camp very miserable. The Serbs had taken control over Bosanski Novi, a small town some twenty kilometres west of Prijedor. Its people had not been crammed into camps. Instead, they had been put on to a column of buses, lorries, and privately owned vehicles, and escorted further north across the Croatian border. By the end of the day, they had reached Karlovac and safety. I was glad that they had not had to go through the same ordeal we Muslims and Croats of Prijedor were experiencing at that time, but Hamdija was really bitter.

'I'm sick and tired of these rotten compromises that the world's political leaders have been making,' he said. 'One day it's going to destroy the whole world. And these Serbs — couldn't they have dealt with us the way they just did with the people of Bosanski Novi? Now that they are in shit up to their necks, having killed so many of us, they can't let us go. Wouldn't it have been better if they had expelled us, too — leaving us some dignity?'

But nobody wanted us. We seemed to be a burden to all sides. Nobody wanted us, but we still hoped to live. I thought: 'Why give up all hope? Why should we accept death as something inevitable?' But not many shared this feeling. Even those with a very strong faith in God had retreated from it. They felt betrayed. On the other hand, I started praying. I prayed for myself, for Kasim and Mama, and after that for some of those who were already dead. I vaguely remembered some of the prayers that Mama had taught me when I was six years old. I would close my eyes, imagining that I lay on the grass surrounded by big, old trees. It was dark. The moon was full. The trees had no shadows. Kasim lay next to me. We would try to sleep. I prayed and prayers would help me erect a low fence around us. No one could step over it. No intruder could enter into our enclosure. It was defended by invisible guardians summoned up by my prayers. We were safe inside the fence.

At times, I would have an eerie feeling that all this was definitely not happening to us.

'Maybe it isn't true, maybe it's a hallucination,' I wondered. But the smell of excrement from the blocked sinks assured me it *was* reality.

Sitting in that corner, I thought about other similar situations. Lebanon, Angola, Romania. Before, I would watch the news on TV about what had been happening there — and then I would switch the TV off and continue my everyday business thinking: 'There's nothing I can do about it.'

After the chaos in Romania in 1989, it had occurred to me for the first time that there existed the possibility of a conflict at home — where the overall situation was not at its best. I became frightened. But for all my forebodings I certainly never expected, not even remotely, that events in Bosnia might take the shape of what was actually happening now. Instead of the smaller fires that had swept through the Romanian cities, Bosnian towns were now caught up in one huge inferno. I was also thinking: 'Yesterday Lebanon, Angola, Romania; today Bosnia, and inevitably tomorrow some other country. But it never lasts forever. There's a point when every conflict comes to an end. This one will stop one day, too, and somebody always survives. Every conflict has its survivors who live to tell their story, and I will survive this one.'

This helped me not to break down. It helped me to carry on until the next day. The most important thing was to survive today.

Not every piece of news on the radio was bad or disappointing. Taking an interest in sports results may seem inappropriate for such a place, but we did just the same. Heated discussions and arguments developed. One of the first such disputes was over the fact that the Yugoslav team, which would have actually represented Serbia, was denied entrance into the European Football Championship in Sweden. Denmark, which had entered the Championship instead of Yugoslavia, looked like getting into the finals. Speculations were rife.

'What would have happened if the Yugoslav team had remained the old, *real* Yugoslav team as it was before the break-up? Surely we would be the Champions.' The guys who were very keen on sports had something to talk about for days.

The Wimbledon Championships were followed with the same excitement. 'Ivanisevic beat Lendl! Ivanisevic beat Edberg! Ivanisevic beat Sampras!'

This was the year of the summer Olympic Games in Barcelona. The sports maniacs had waited for this event for four years, and now look what had happened. They had no access to a TV. They wanted to get out before the start of the Olympics. They never gave a thought to the fact that their homes had been burnt and their TV sets sold somewhere in Serbia. If they ever got to free territory, they would be sent out to fight — not to watch the Olympics. But it was a welcome distraction. It gave us something to look forward to. If there was nothing you still wanted to live for, then your chances of survival became very slim.

Hamdija became my best friend. We talked very little about sports. Our conversations ranged from discussing the current political situation to me teaching him English. We daydreamed about going to Germany or Sweden and working there on a remote farm.

When Hamdija would return to his place, I would continue living on the farm in my head. The farm was not mine, but there were no other people around. I was alone. The cows were big, clean and beautiful. Their skin was a mixture of brown and white. They were milk cows, not cows fed for slaughter. They grazed in a field surrounded by a wooden fence. When I fed them in the sheds, they did not push each other around. They waited quietly for me to put hay before them. At the end of the day, I would be very tired. I would have a shower and then go to my small room. I did not eat. I felt no need for food. I would light a lamp and sit on the bed. The bed was small and simple. It had hand-woven bedding with beautiful coloured stripes.

A whole day would pass and I would not utter a word. Even the cows did not moo. The silence was deep. There were no other houses or farms around. There were no roads. No traffic. I was all alone, but I was not lonely.

When winter came to the farm, it was time for me to go back to the world. I left with two shirts, two pairs of trousers, one jacket, a pair of docker shoes, a woollen cap (as my head was shaven), and a small personal hygiene kit. I packed my rucksack and left the world of tranquillity behind.

I was often accompanied by Hamdija in these daydreams. With Kasim, he talked about fishing. They had fished together many times. He was crazy about it and Kasim was a real fishing maniac.

Hamdija was once approached by a guard with whom some years before he had attended a work re-training programme in Sarajevo. They had never met again, but this guard had not forgotten him. He would call Hamdija out of the room from time to time, and he would give him a nice, fresh piece of bread. A couple of times, he brought green peppers and gherkins. Hamdija shared this bounty with Kasim and me. While we were eating, other guys were asking each other: 'What's that smell? Is it gherkins?' They seemed to think they were imagining things.

My gums were bleeding heavily, and the crust of the several-days-old bread was as sharp as the edge of a knife. Eating was torture. Hamdija would give me that nice, soft bread and he would eat my old bread instead. In these conditions, where everybody was forced to look after only himself, his generosity moved me. Once the guard gave Hamdija a whole cigarette. Hamdija came to us and produced the cigarette with a smile.

'Where did you get it from?' Kasim and I also had broad smiles on our faces.

All money was long gone, and people around us smoked dried meadow grass and blackberry leaves — which they would quickly gather while they used the fields as a toilet.

The most wonderful contact I had with the outside world was not radio news, but a message I received in my sleep. Mama came to comfort her children in this tragedy.

It was early morning with the first signs of daybreak, and a thick fog was all around. She stood in the field in which I used to play with other children. Between us, there was a road and a giant oak tree. I used to sit beneath this oak on my way back from school — especially if I had been tired out by playing football after classes. Mama looked very calm and she spoke to me softly — like when a mother whispers to her baby: *'Don't worry about anything, darling. Everything is going to be all right.'*

I believed in this dream. It made a huge impact on my camp life. I believed her. Kasim and I *would* be all right. Even when I could hear people being tortured and killed beneath the window of my room, I clung to this dream. At these moments, a hush would descend on the room. We all sat transfixed with terror. The same fear which I felt could be seen in everybody's eyes. This dream was somehow a glimmer of light at the end of the dark tunnel that was Omarska.

14

The guards had no records of people kept in the camp. They kept no evidence of those tortured and executed. Often they killed without knowing who the victims were, or where they came from, or what their 'crimes' had supposedly been. The executions often took place in the 'Red House' after interrogations. Some of those who had been beaten were taken, still alive, out of the interrogation offices and left on the 'pista' to die shortly afterwards in the scorching sun. Those still able to speak always pleaded for some water — but their pleas remained unanswered. All of us sitting on the 'pista' dared not even look at them. But most often, killings took place in the big garage and on the grass around the 'White House'. Sometimes they took place at other locations — sometimes outside the camp, too.

The radiator fixed to the wall next to my shower cubicle became a kind of witness stand for a number of these atrocities. A mixture of curiosity and anxiety tempted almost everyone in the showers to have a look out of the small window above the radiator. The radiator was like a magnet, and the feet of those standing on it were drawn to its surface. It was difficult for the guards to notice them, because only a pair of eyes and the top of a head would show over the sill. At first, most people would say: 'Get down! Get down! They'll kill us all!' But the one standing at the window would remain there transfixed. After a while, everybody would ask: 'What's going on? What can you see?'

Those bearing witness to the scenes outside sometimes recognised the victim or the executioner — or both. Sometimes they knew neither. I never wanted to look outside. Having to listen to what was happening behind the wall was already too much for me. One day Zahid was feeling the heat badly, and he stood next to the window trying to catch some fresh air. The Chetniks were calling somebody to come out of the 'White House' — but their victim persistently remained inside. When they failed to reassure him that they meant no harm, their calls turned to shouts. Zahid climbed up on the radiator. We almost screamed at him to get down, but he was kept there by the hand of some invisible force and nothing could bring him away from his perch. When we realised he was not coming down, he was bombarded with a wave of questions.

'What is it? What's happening? What can you see? What is it?'

He was staring out and not a single word came out of him. It was as if he had been hypnotised. The sounds outside suggested some sort of struggle was going on. A voice was screaming and there was loud laughter. Then there was a short burst of gunfire. Zahid stepped down and sighed deeply, 'Oh, my God, what they did to that poor man.'

'What happened, what happened?' everybody asked.

'They grabbed his legs trying to drag him out of the "White House". He was screaming and trying to hold on to something. When he grabbed the doorstep they fired across his back.' A deadly silence filled the showers.

Kasim was one of those who climbed up on to the radiator. At first, it was because he wanted to identify our friends and neighbours among the inmates from the small room in the garage who would sit in front of the 'White House' after a meal. This was often the only way of seeing if somebody was missing. But after Drazenko Predojevic had started picking on him, and after many inmates said they had admitted to the interrogators that they knew he had had a rifle, he began to climb on to the radiator out of anxiety.

It was in this way that Kasim witnessed a man being killed by Marinko 'Pavin' Jokic in broad daylight. Pavin took his victim to the edge of the 'pista' outside the 'White House'. There was nobody else around but the two of them. Pavin started beating the man with his truncheon. The man was just groaning. After a while, he fell on the ground — but Pavin kept hitting him. The victim soon stopped showing any signs of life. Pavin sat down, lit a cigarette, and had a break. When he had finished his cigarette, he resumed the beating — even though it was clear that the man was already dead.

I kept asking Kasim not to take any such risk of exposing himself unnecessarily to the danger of being seen — but he could not resist the temptation. He could not sleep — and as I started warning him more and more often, he changed his tactics and looked outside when I was asleep.

In the evenings, the Chetniks would regularly make an inmate chop some wood and light a fire for them on the grass between the 'White House' and the 'Red House'. They would sit next to it drinking plum brandy. Usually they would kill several people, too. One morning after I woke up, Kasim told me about the scene he had witnessed the previous evening. He recognised the victim, who was from Jakupovici. He was beaten with iron rods and rifle butts. While he was crying, the torturers were laughing. When they had had enough, they nailed him through his chest to the ground with a long iron rod. Kasim could not keep these scenes to himself. He had to tell me about them.

I could see that the anxiety Kasim felt was shared by some of those who came to talk to him. Nail Jakupovic was one of them. Kasim and he talked, and I listened. Nail seemed calm. He talked about German beer. Work in Germany had helped him build a new house. The last time we saw our village, his old house had been reduced to a pile of ash. The new one had been turned into a burning torch. It soon turned out that this was the source of his anxiety. He felt specially targeted. He and his son, Sead, were repeatedly taken for interrogations and beaten. He asked Kasim what had happened at his interrogation.

'They know I had arms,' Kasim sighed.

'They accused Sead and me of organising resistance.' Nail's voice turned into a whisper. He was clearly upset. It was not the German beer but his anxiety that brought him to Kasim. He needed to talk, to confide in someone. Kasim was safe to talk to as he was in the same predicament, and he would also keep it all to himself. Nail felt another man in similar trouble would understand him best. But his son, Sead, kept to himself. He never talked to anybody, and each time the door opened his eyes would turn towards it as if he was waiting for the guards to come and take him away.

When Nail was brought back from his last interrogation, he became as quiet as his son. From then on, he refused to go for meals. When Kasim tried to get him to go to the canteen — for he could not survive for very long without food — he just shook his head. Soon after, both of them were taken out and nobody ever saw them again.

Many inmates were murdered for private reasons. Guards who had a grudge against somebody took their revenge. The 'visitors' from outside often took advantage of the same opportunity. Every Serb had a licence to kill. They could come in whenever they wanted and kill whomever they pleased, especially as their leaders and superiors from Prijedor and Banja Luka sanctioned this activity. As we had been judged disposable, the precise method of our removal was irrelevant.

Sakib Pervanic, a thirty-two-year-old from my village, 'disappeared' because of an old grudge against his father. Sakib's father, Mustafa, had had business deals with Rade Gruban — but over the years they had failed to settle some business debts. Rade owned a couple of small grocery shops also selling home appliances. One of the shops was in my village. The business was going well and he decided to expand it through bulk sales of cement, but he did not have the necessary storage space. Mustafa let him a part of his basement for this purpose, but they could not agree on the amount of the rent. As a result, Mustafa refused to pay Rade for some appliances he had purchased on credit. Rade now wanted revenge — but Mustafa was in the Trnopolje camp. It saved him, but not his son.

One morning in late July, at about 2.00am, the guards opened the door.

'Sakib Pervanic,' Soskan shouted, 'come out here.' Silence.

'We know you're in here. You have nothing to fear, we won't harm you.'

'He's not in here,' somebody answered.

Sakib first looked confused, then petrified. The guards left. Samir and Jasmin tried to calm him down. Five minutes later, the guards were back.

'We know you're in here,' they called. He could not hide for they knew he was in the camp. At first, they just did not know in which room he was kept. Now, somebody from the small room inside the garage had told them he was in here, and he had to go out.

The night was humid and sticky, and Sakib slept in a T-shirt and shorts. While he was dressing, Samir and Fikret went to the door and talked to their friend Soskan. Everyone else was quiet. We all knew Sakib was going to be 'exchanged'. The slowness with which he put his clothes on, his slow walk past those sitting on the floor — delaying the moment of leaving the room — showed that the words he had spoken earlier were probably just thoughtless words of temporary desperation. He had claimed he would rather be killed than tortured psychologically and exposed to deliberate starvation.

'Why don't they throw a couple of hand grenades inside the room and bring this torture to an end?' he had said.

We all suffered, but I did not want to be ripped to pieces by hand grenades. I clung to the belief that this could not go on forever.

'Don't say that,' I said. 'If you feel like dying, there is the field behind the "White House". You can run into it and get shot every day when we go for a meal.' He just kept his head down.

Maybe in those moments, Sakib just lacked the spirit to fight and endure. Or perhaps since Rade was looking for his father, he feared that this dreadful moment could come any time.

'Don't hurt him,' Samir said to Soskan, 'he's my brother.'

'Is he your real brother?' Soskan asked.

'He's my aunt's son.'

'Don't worry. Nobody will hurt him.'

Sakib stepped outside. The door closed.

This scenario had taken place many times before this night. I knew where this journey would take Sakib. We all knew that being taken out to be 'exchanged' for a Serbian prisoner, in fact, meant summary execution. It was painful to witness such moments, but thinking too much about it created an enemy within — an enemy that could invade your mind and make you its prisoner. To survive, it was essential to suppress its awakening. The best way of doing this, even though it was quite difficult, was to quickly turn your mind away from what had just happened.

15

Kasim's birthday was coming up, and I kept catching myself
thinking of this occasion. A few times, I almost mentioned
it to him, as I found it very hard to keep these thoughts to
myself. The day came and I remained silent. What could I have
told him? Happy birthday, brother? I thought of this particular day
and compared it with all the other days we had spent in the camp.
Yesterday was gone, and the people we were yesterday were no
more. We lived one day only — today. We lived like butterflies.
Every morning we were born, and we could only hope to live until
the end of the day. Life throughout the night was the life of a larva,
frightened that the guards might come to the room and break the
safety of its cocoon. If it was lucky, the next morning the larva
would break free of its cocoon and the butterfly would emerge
hoping to live another day. I wished I could say to Kasim, 'Happy
birthday, my brother butterfly.' I wished I could say the same each
day until the day of our freedom — the day when I would tell him,

'Happy birthday, brother. Today you are born as a man. Today is the first day of the rest of your life. I wish you to wake up on many mornings after this one and repeat to yourself: *Today is the first day of the rest of my life.*' My brother never knew about the thoughts I had had on his birthday.

Months later at the Manjaca camp, Ibrahim Pervanic revealed to Kasim and me that when Sakib failed to respond to the guards' first call they went to the small room in the garage. They called Sakib's name, and Ibrahim went to the door and said to them: 'He's not in here.'

'We know he's in the camp. We saw him.'

'He's not in here,' Ibrahim repeated. While talking to them, Ibrahim glanced at the list one of them had in his hand. Ibrahim's name was below Sakib's. There were more Pervanic surnames, all typed in red ink. But after Sakib was taken out, something unexpected happened. The Serbs brought to the camp a large number of people from Brdo — a hilly region west of Prijedor which contained several villages. Suddenly, the camp authorities shifted their priority from liquidation of the people whose names were typed in red ink to mass executions of the new arrivals. While Ibrahim was telling us this compelling story, I had a quick flashback to my dream and to the message Mama had brought me in that dream — *Everything is going to be all right.*

We survived, but many men from Brdo died. Their arrival in the last week of July marked the beginning of the period of mass executions by firearms. For many days after the fall of Hambarine, the Chetniks did not penetrate further inside the territory inhabited by the Muslims of Brdo. When 'cleansing' of the Kozarac area had ended, the Chetniks concentrated all their efforts on 'cleansing' the inhabitants of Brdo. It all started on July 20 and was already finished by the 23rd. This 'cleansing' wiped out almost the entire population. The Chetniks went from house to house, slitting the throats of people of all ages. Several thousand people had died on their doorsteps before an order to stop this slaughter was given.

Survivors of this carnage were separated — men were taken to Omarska and Keraterm, and women and children ended up in Trnopolje.

With their arrival, the camp became crammed once again. For the first time, firearms were used for mass executions. At night the camp guards would take out whole groups of people from Brdo. Just metres away from the executions, I could hear the guards saying: 'Run,' and then a round of machine-gun fire.

This was a new experience for us, the old Omarska inmates. There had been no mass executions by firearms until now. The killing of such a large number of people every night raised many questions. Why this sudden change? Are they in a hurry to get rid of us all? Is it going to be our turn next?

The chances of escape were nil, but one evening, somebody did escape. All hell broke loose. The guards were running up and down the wide field behind the 'White House', but he was gone. The fugitive was still fresh and strong, so he could run fast. A tractor with a spotlight was used to no avail. Next morning, a 'hunting squad' made up of six Chetniks went in search of him. Hours later, they were back empty-handed. His cousins, relatives, and neighbours were less fortunate.

Executions now claimed on average one hundred lives every night. This lasted for about ten days. The bodies of the dead were simply dumped behind the 'White House'. Every morning, members of the working unit had to load them on the yellow lorry driven by Vlado Kobas — another former neighbour.

Arrival of the men from Brdo may have saved some others, but it did not save Prijedor's intellectuals. Judges, lawyers, computer experts, doctors, teachers, managers — they all perished in this last week of July. They were the victims of the Serbian plan for the systematic extermination of all non-Serbian elements capable of and likely to play an active role in the revival of any sort of economic or social life. Three of them were with us in the showers: Stjepan 'Stipe' Maric, Esad 'Eso' Mehmedagic, and Ibrahim 'Ibro' Paunovic.

The first one to go was Stipe — a slim, short civil servant from Prijedor. He was married to a Serb who worked as a nurse, and with whom he had had two small children. He was charged with compiling lists of Serb children chosen for termination. He was not aware of his 'crime' until Zeljko Marmat, who specialised in terminating Croat inmates, took Stipe out. It was late in the evening. Seconds later, we heard voices coming from the big garage under the room. They were loud, aggressive, accusing voices — and Stipe's voice sounded defensive. This was followed by loud screams. The room went quiet with a chilly silence. We stared at each other, but nobody said a word. The shouts and cries lasted a long time. The unasked question hung in the air. Is he coming back or not?

Badly beaten, with deep cuts on his legs, Stipe did come back. Accusing him of having taken part in a conspiracy organised to kill Serb children, Marmat demanded half a million German marks to spare his life. Stipe did not have any savings, and Marmat lowered his demand to fifty thousand. Stipe did not have this money either. A week later, he was called out for an 'exchange'.

'Stjepan Maric,' a guard called from the door.

'Here.' Stipe anxiously stood up and went to the door.

'You're going for an exchange. Take all your possessions and come outside.'

Stipe tried to remain calm. He left his blanket behind — a blanket which had been sent to him by his Serbian wife — along with some biscuits which he had freely shared with us. He took his jacket, and saying goodbye to all of us in the showers, he left the room.

Stipe was a nice man who always had words of consolation for those cracking under pressure. When Sakib would moan, as if he were the only one in trouble, Stipe told him the story of a former Russian prisoner — a victim of Stalin's purges. This man had survived seventeen years of imprisonment in Siberia. On his release, he wrote a book about his fight for survival. He lived for some years after his release. The point Stipe was trying to make was that no matter how long our imprisonment was going to last — weeks, months, or years — once you give up the fight you are finished. Stipe was a fighter, but the Chetniks gave him no chance.

Just days after Stipe's departure it was Eso's turn. Eso was a retired judge and the former president of the court in Prijedor. He was ninety-seven per cent blind, yet he was accused of being a sniper. The poor man needed someone to lead him to the toilet. He had tried to send messages to his wife through Miroslav Zoric, my former teacher and interrogator. Eso's wife was still at home in Prijedor, and in these messages Eso had asked her to go and see a friend — a member of the Serb Crisis Committee whom he believed would get him out of here. I believe that all Eso's messages ended up in the rubbish bin.

'I'm innocent,' poor Eso would say. 'They have no reason to keep me in here.'

We were all innocent, but as an intellectual he was in greater danger than most of us. Finally, he was taken out. It was sunny outside and Eso stood up thinking his friend had helped him to be released. The call from the door brought a smile back to his face. The poor man thought he was going home. Ibro, who throughout the whole period of detention had looked after Eso, helped the aged 'sniper' once more to find his way to the door. A minute or two later, a couple of shots came from the direction of the 'Red House'.

This same afternoon, Prijedor's ousted mayor, Muhamed Cehajic, was taken out after Eso. Ceno, a neighbour from my village, heard a guard who was taking Cehajic towards the 'Red House' say to him: 'Mayor, the place we are taking you to will be much better than the one you are leaving. You'll have your own bed, more food, and good washing facilities ...' Ceno did not hear the rest as the pair walked away from his window.

Soon after Cehajic, it was the turn of criminal inspector Mirso. All together, almost fifty intellectuals and civic leaders died that afternoon and in the night that followed.

16

A couple of days after Eso's death, the routine was broken. We did not go to the canteen. The guards came to the door and ordered us to lie down facing the floor — hands clasped behind our backs. They warned us to keep quiet. All conversation died away instantly. It was unusual because it happened in broad daylight. Usually we were made to lie like this in the evenings, when the guards came to pick out shoes and trainers that they liked. Eventually, we found out that foreign reporters had come to visit the camp.

Several days before this visit, a group of men had been selected to go to the Kozarac area to collect remains of the bodies of people and animals still lying there. They said that the stench had been unbearable, for the bodies were badly deteriorated after long exposure to hot weather. They had had to collect the remains with their bare hands. As soon as they had tried to lift them, the bodies would fall apart. When the Chetniks had realised it was not possible to do the job this way, they had provided some blankets and bed-sheets into which the bodies could be rolled. Some bodies had been torn apart by dogs scavenging for food. The Chetniks wanted to clean the area before the foreign reporters' arrival. They did not want them to take pictures of their crimes.

The Chetniks went through the room selecting groups of men who looked better physically than the rest of us. These men were presented to the foreign cameras as the only inmates inside the camp. They were taken to the canteen and given the kind of food we had never seen before. It was nothing extravagant. But the plates were topped with cooked beans. Each man was given quarter of a loaf of bread.

The days preceding this visit had been unusually quiet. The killings had stopped completely. Suddenly, the guards became 'nice' to us — switching almost instantly from terror and torture to something resembling their behaviour in the first days of the camp's existence. They allowed us to go to other rooms and visit our friends and neighbours. Rumours started spreading that the camp was to close in a matter of days. I realised that what Ibro Paunovic had told us a couple of nights earlier might turn out to be true. Pirvan had taken Ibro to the guards' room. They had explained to him that they planned to close the camp, because they had to put the mine back into production within the next three weeks. Ibro had been the technical director of the mine. They had offered him beer and left him sitting there while they chatted amongst themselves and listened to the music on the radio. When he came back, he laughed at the idea of opening the mine within the following three weeks. For various reasons, that would be impossible. But he also came back convinced that some major change would take place soon. Unfortunately, he did not live to witness it himself. Two nights after his conversation with the guards, they took him out again. I heard several steps on the stairs, and a blunt blow followed by a scream. Ibro was no more.

The morning was glorious. The sun was already well above the horizon. After the reporters left, the guards took us to the canteen. Sitting on the grass after the meal, I saw a large group — about two hundred and fifty men — being rushed out of their room. They had been brought from Keraterm late the night before. Most of the inmates who had survived Keraterm were transferred to the Trnopolje camp. Unfortunately for these men, they had been chosen for termination.

'Shall we take them to eat?' one of the guards asked his colleague.

'If there's enough food.'

Kasim recognised several men from Keraterm. Some of them looked sadly in our direction. Their eyes said more than all the words in this world could ever say. They seemed to be isolated in some way. It was as if a barrier of thick glass stood between us. We sensed and they sensed that they were about to embark on their last journey. A young boy was sitting on a concrete block on the corner of the administration building. He kept his head down. Blood was pouring out of his mouth. His cheeks were swollen. Then an order arrived: 'Put them on the buses.' They were put on to two buses which left immediately. No one from this group was ever seen again.

In the afternoon, the guards asked if any of us had any barber skills. For some reason, they wanted us to have a haircut. Two men from my village, Senad Sivac and Bahrija Jakupovic, volunteered for this job. The guards then selected several others at random, and took them to the room next to the toilet. Goran Gruban and another guard stood at the door keeping an eye on them. They laughed and played a game of aiming their rifles at the men in the room. The trick was to pull the trigger as far as possible without firing. But Goran miscalculated and shot Senad in the neck. Bahrija was then sent back to the room. I was deeply shocked. Even in this place, disbelief swept through the room. Everybody wanted to know exactly what had happened. Bahrija was very pale and frightened, as if he had just had an encounter with a ghost.

Senad was wrapped in a blanket and placed outside by the entrance door. One Chetnik went to the canteen, and moments later he came back followed by 'Cvitonja' Pavlic. Pavlic pulled out his automatic pistol and fired twice. All of this happened just a couple of metres from my shower cubicle. Only the wall stood between us. I realised Senad was dead. Senad's father, Refik, had been sitting on the grass — just a couple of metres away from him. But neither he nor anybody else could determine the identity of the person in the blanket.

Senad had never believed that he would get out alive. 'We'll never get out of here,' he would say, with more sadness than bitterness in his voice.

'Of course we will,' I would tell him. 'It may take years, but it has to come to an end.' My optimism did not change his mood.

I often talked to him about other things — things from our previous life — just to draw his attention away from the events taking place around us. This afternoon was the first time I had seen him cheerful.

Senad was daring. In the canteen, he would pour two plates of soup into one. The empty plate had to be placed quickly beneath the full one. To escape the watchful eyes of the guards, this had to be done in a fraction of a second. In the canteen Senad's reflexes never let him down. This afternoon, they could not help him to escape the bullet.

The following day, not long after the meal, when everybody was back in the room, the guards started shouting.

'Everybody out. Quickly.'

We left the room, and again sat on the grass before the 'White House'. Everybody, the whole camp, was outside. Three or four Chetniks carried some papers around. Soon a bus arrived and stopped on the 'pista'. A group of thirty-one women came out of the canteen and got on to the bus. Ten to fifteen minutes later, the bus left. Nobody knew where they were being taken. Six women remained in the camp. Hajra Hadzic, a young shoe factory worker from Kozarac, and Jadranka Gavranovic remained in the 'White House'. Sadeta Medunjanin, the wife of the murdered Becir Medunjanin; a woman called Zdena; Sebiha Kahrimanovic; and Mevlida Mahmuljin, a teacher and SDA activist from Kozarac, were still in the canteen.

The Chetniks holding the papers announced they were going to read out our names. Those called out were to gather on the 'pista'. The whole procedure was very confusing and disorganised. The Chetnik reading out the names was not prepared to read them again if his pronunciation was not correct. He found it impossible to pronounce names that contained 'h'. People who had been killed long before — even those already transferred to Trnopolje weeks earlier — were being called out. The Chetniks simply had not kept any evidence of the number of people in the camp. They did not have a clue as to who they had killed and who was still alive. Obviously, the interrogators had not even bothered to cross out the names of those killed during interrogations.

We were divided into two groups — nobody knew why. If we had known that those called out first were being sent to the Trnopolje camp, those who had wanted to go there could have answered in place of those who were now dead.

The roll-call took about two hours. In the end, about six hundred were chosen for transfer to Trnopolje. Kasim and I remained in the larger group of some 1,350. The roll-call more or less confirmed my previous calculation that at least three thousand inmates had vanished for ever. The greatest number had been killed in the Chetniks' night orgies and in the daily interrogations. Every day, up to July 22, there had been between thirty and forty bodies set out on the grass behind the 'White House'. After that date, with the arrival of the men from Brdo and for the next ten days, about 1,000 lives had been lost. Several hundred had been taken for alleged exchanges which never took place. Less than two thousand of us were still alive.

When this first selection was finished, our group was ordered to go to the rear garage. The guards pushed us inside like a herd of cattle. The place soon became jam-packed. A few new Chetniks stood on a dumper lorry. I recognised one of them, but did not know his name. During the years I had spent in the primary school in Omarska, he had worked at the police station. Now he ranked amongst the high police officials. The noise of bus engines started and a policeman shouted at us: 'Everybody listen! When I call your name, say *here* very loudly, and go out to one of the buses.'

The first roll-call had lasted almost two hours. This one was going to take more than six. They seemed to have realised this themselves. After the first ten to fifteen minutes, the roll-call stopped. The police officials standing on the lorry had a short exchange. Then they separated a hundred and seventy-four men at random. They were taken to one of the smaller rooms on the first floor. The purpose of this separation was not explained. Then we were told: 'The rest of you run outside and get on the buses.'

On the way to the buses, we passed those six hundred men on the 'pista'. They were still sitting on the tarmac, keeping their heads down. Two Chetniks standing at the front door of my bus were swearing and beating everybody who was getting in. When we were seated, they ordered us to keep our heads down and not to look out of the windows.

One Chetnik asked an inmate whom he obviously recognised: 'Do you know me?'

'Yes, I do,' the man replied.

'Where from?'

'We did our National Service together.'

'You damned motherfucker.' The Chetnik grabbed the walking

stick this man used for support and started hitting him with it. The man raised his hands to protect his face.

'Yes, motherfucker — we did serve together. So why didn't you join me in the fight in Croatia?'

'My sister is married to a Serb. My brother-in-law was fighting in Croatia.'

'If you're innocent, why didn't he come to help you? He could've done it if he'd wanted to.' The men said nothing.

There were not enough seats for all of us. People were still being herded in. In the end, the bus was overcrowded. At the back, a group of men were forced to lie on each other. One of them moaned at the bottom of the pile. The Chetnik went back to him, hitting everyone around him with the truncheon and the stick which he had taken from his first victim. I kept my head down. The blows made some people cry out, and this enraged him further. He went berserk. The sounds of beating and swearing made me keep my head even lower. On his way back to the front, he hit Kasim on the head with the truncheon. All the muscles on Kasim's face contracted in pain — but he kept quiet.

'Everybody wearing anything green — take it off and throw it out of the window.' Shirts and T-shirts flew out of the window.

'This too?' I stood up and showed my T-shirt — which was now dirty yellow with a greenish tinge.

'Yes,' he said. I took it off and pushed it through the window above my seat. I saw people still boarding the other buses.

'Off your seats! Sit on the floor facing the seats. Keep your heads down.'

We were squashed between seats, but still had to make more space. The passage between the seats was full. The last ones entering the bus had to walk over those in the passage and pile up on top of them. It is hard to understand how all those men did not suffocate during the journey that followed. The Chetniks were rather amused by the whole situation. Laughing, they kept saying:

'Bring more of them over here. There's still some space left.'

The voice of the same man who had been moaning before could be heard once again. He had several men on top of him. He was asking them not to press too much — but there was nothing they could do about it. The bully Chetnik screamed at him to stop moaning, but he paid no attention. This enraged the bully so much that he walked over several layers of men on the floor, and upon reaching the back of the bus, he beat everyone savagely.

I was on the far side next to the window in the worst possible place of all. Those in the middle squeezed me against the side. I could not breathe. I quietly asked some of the men next to Kasim to give me a bit more space, but they did not budge. The pain in my knees was unbearable. I could not move my legs at all. I managed to push my blanket on to the floor. It was very hot. There was no air in the bus and I sweated profusely. Sweat kept pouring down my face, and my hair was all wet. I feared I would become dehydrated. Not a single drop of water was available. On top of it all, I was stupid enough to chew a piece of bread, thinking it would make me feel better. It made me even more thirsty. If I had possessed the whole world in those moments I would have exchanged it for just one glass of water.

The column of buses started to move. Those six hundred who remained behind us were still sitting on the 'pista'. Nobody knew where we were heading. Outside the main camp gates, the column stopped for a couple of moments on the flyover. I could not see the crowd outside, but could clearly hear them shouting.

'Kill them! Kill them all!'

We moved off again. All the time we were entertained by our escorts. Before reaching the final destination, we had screwed Alija (Izetbegovic) and Alija had screwed us one million times.

'You voted for him and for the independent Bosnia,' they were cursing us. 'Where's your Bosnia now? It's no bigger than a *fildzan*.' Fildzan was a very small coffee cup without a handle.

All I knew was that the column was moving east. We were forced to sing Chetnik nationalistic songs. If our singing was not to our escorts' and driver's taste, they shouted: 'Louder, louder.' If they liked it, we had to repeat it over and over again. For one of these songs, nobody knew the lyrics. We all kept quiet.

'What are you waiting for? Why aren't you singing?' They were confused by our disobedience.

'We don't know the words,' we said.

'They don't know the words,' one of them said sarcastically. 'Then we'll teach you the words. All right? Repeat after me: "Alija, Alija, if there be war".'

All of us in one voice repeated after him: 'Alija, Alija, if there be war.' He carried on: 'I'll slit your throat, I'll slit your throat, just like Milos did Murat's.' And we repeated it in unison. He repeated the lyrics once more and we sang like nightingales.

Suddenly, the column stopped. I could not feel my legs any more. I was soaked in sweat. The Chetniks left the bus, having warned everybody not to move. Those at the front door saw the Chetniks standing outside the local shop, drinking beer. They were waiting for somebody or something. Forty minutes later, a new group of Chetniks arrived and the journey continued.

I started believing we were heading for a real exchange. The sun was setting slowly. Just before dark, the column was passing between mobs of mad Serbs on both sides who were hurling stones, clods of earth, and God knows what else at us. The column kept moving. After some seven hours, the journey ended on a mountain plateau. I strongly believed it was Vlasic Mountain in Central Bosnia.

'With daybreak our side will arrive and we'll be exchanged,' I hoped. This hope was reinforced when I heard the words: 'The Lieutenant-Colonel won't take in any of them before they've had a medical check-up.'

After midnight, they took an old man out of my bus. He came

back to collect money, jewellery, and watches. Most of it had already been seized in Omarska, but some men still had a few things. The old man was crying: 'More, folks, more. They'll kill me if I don't collect more of it.' Somebody said: 'Tell them we already gave everything to the guards in Omarska.' He left and seconds later we heard laughter.

'They already cleaned them out in Omarska.'

They instantly knew it was true, and they let the old man come back on the bus. The journey was exhausting and we were all dehydrated. Some men licked drops of moisture running down the windows.

Later in the night, the Chetniks again came to the bus. They were looking for some men — Jasmin 'Jamo' Alisic, Dedo Crnalic — a well-known businessman from Prijedor, Nezir Krak, Nedzad 'Djuzin' Babic, and several others. None of them were on our bus. The sounds of questioning and beating could soon be heard — indicating they had managed to find some of them. The morning revealed that these men had been murdered during the night. Some of those they had been looking for had managed to hide in the dark, but they were found in the morning when we disembarked from the buses. They found them all. I heard: 'There you are, Jamo. Come over here, my friend.' They were taken behind some farming machinery and had their throats slit.

With daylight, I realised this was not to be an exchange. We were brought to the Manjaca camp. The Manjaca guards stood there without interfering. Outside the wire, we were anybody's game. Anybody could kill us without having to answer for it. Inside the wire, it was a different story.

Part Three

———

Manjaca

17

The misty mountain air was filled with the fresh smell of wild mint flowers. The whole plateau was a huge purple carpet. The place was hell, but it smelt like paradise. Drops of dew covering the wild flowers shone like the clearest diamonds. Parched men licked the dew. In the East, the sun was rising. The only things spoiling this idyllic picture were canons, anti-aircraft missiles and the Chetniks.

It turned out that more of us had been brought to Manjaca than the camp authorities had expected to settle inside the wire. They indicated that some of us might be returned to Omarska. All this time, Kasim was telling me that the best safety was behind the barbed wire. I never asked what made him so confident about it, but his prophecy was soon to be fulfilled.

We were sitting on the ground. A camp official known as Sergeant Spaga arrived. He was wearing camouflage fatigues and a red beret. He held lists several pages long.

'Listen, everybody.' The tone of his voice indicated he was not asking for our attention, but issuing a hostile warning. 'Keep quiet, and when I call your name, go on to the road and line up in rows of seven.' A macadam road was between us and the camp wire.

The Chetniks present on the plateau were mixed — they included both our convoy escorts and the Manjaca guards. The latter looked like professional soldiers. Only a few of our escorts were the guards from the Omarska camp. Others, even though from the Prijedor district, were strangers. Several Manjaca guards brought us some water. Just enough for each of us to moisten his dry throat. Others walking between us asked if we had any money.

'Give it to us and we'll keep it safe for you until you are released. We'll issue receipts to every person stating how much money you gave us.'

Incredible though it was, there were a few who had managed to bring some money this far. Frightened by the torture and murder that had taken place on this very plateau when we disembarked, they gave the money away. No one dared ask for a receipt. The money was 'safely' deposited in the shirt pockets of guards hiding their identity behind expensive sun glasses. I have never seen so many Ray Bans in one place — before or since.

Some young men in old army uniforms came out of the camp. They passed us quietly heading down the slope. At the bottom, they cut some green ferns. On the way back, they hid their faces behind the ferns. Neither I nor anybody else from my group knew who they were or what they needed the ferns for.

The process of matching the names from Spaga's lists with the men present on the plateau was a lengthy procedure. The sun was already well above the horizon. The weather was perfect for holidaymakers relaxing on the Mediterranean coasts. Less than thirty minutes by plane from here, tourists were enjoying the sunny beaches of Italy.

Kasim and I were finally called. I was first, and Kasim

followed soon after. Actually, we were lucky to be among the last to be called, because it meant we had to kneel on the road's sharp rubble for a shorter time. Those called first had had to spend the entire period of the roll-call on their knees and elbows — more than three hours.

When the last person had been called, we still had to remain on our knees and elbows, heads bent to the ground, for a long time. The sun was already high up in the sky, scorching us. We could just as easily have lined up standing on the road, or sitting on the ground next to it. What was the purpose of this? What were they trying to achieve? Humiliation? Sadistic pleasure? It was almost impossible to control the pain in the knee caps and the elbows caused by the sharp rubble for longer than fifteen minutes. But every move was punished by a prompt kick in the head or the ribs. Once more, we were forced to sing the same old songs we had sung during the exhausting journey. They also asked provocative questions.

'Would you like to fuck a Serbian woman?' Still remaining in the kneeling position, we had replied: 'No.' It seemed to be the wrong answer.

'So you think Serbian women are not good enough for you? I fucked Muslim women and they were good.' Naturally, no decent human being would say 'yes' — notwithstanding that this too would probably turn out to be the wrong answer.

The sun burned mercilessly, and a stream of sweat was pouring down my face. I would sweep it off with my jumper sleeve, but in seconds new streams of sweat would blind me. I could not take any more of it. I was going to faint. I also noticed that in spite of all the beatings nobody was actually getting killed. So I asked the Chetnik next to me to let me go and urinate. He did. I went towards a group of bushes.

Once I was back in the row, the first thirty men got up and moved inside the wire. On the gates was a wooden sign with the word 'camp' on it, written in Cyrillic script. Close to the gates, young soldiers were preparing food in a mobile army cauldron. I kept looking at the cauldron.

'We'll get soup,' I thought. 'We're going to sleep inside these bungalows.' I was looking at several small buildings on the left side of the road. 'They can't accommodate us all if they put beds in there. The floor is probably covered with light army mattresses to provide enough space for everyone. After Omarska, this place is going to be a five-star Sheraton.'

I could not see anyone moving inside the camp. It was because on this day other Manjaca inmates had remained confined inside their sheds. The same young men who had carried the ferns earlier on could now be seen carrying heavy sacks of cement. There were no signs of communication between them. I still did not know who they were. They just glanced at us with curiosity on their short journey from the bungalow back to the lorry.

We were ordered to sit in front of the first bungalow. Several camp guards left, saying they would bring us some drinking water. It all made me feel better. There were indications that we might be in for a different kind of treatment in here. I did not care about the Geneva Convention and the treatment to which prisoners should be entitled. The hope that my life would be spared for some time was enough.

A water bowser arrived. After the first round, in which each one of us was permitted to drink just a little, everybody was allowed to drink as much as they wanted. In the space of about half an hour, I had more than three litres of ice-cold water.

We were moved across the road. We had to remove belts and shoe laces. The camp rules permitted the use of improvised laces if we managed to find something to serve this purpose inside the wire — with a maximum length of fifteen centimetres. Anybody caught with something longer was severely punished for breaching the camp rules. From here, in pairs, we went inside the infirmary — a small room inside one of the bungalows. The room contained no medical equipment. There was a desk and a civilian doctor. A guard at the door ordered me to strip down to my underwear, to take everything out of my bag, and to empty all my pockets. Sejo, a neighbour from Kevljani, retained some documents in his bag — with immediate consequences. The guard delivered two punches to his stomach, shouting: 'Didn't you understand what I said?'

In the morning, when I saw the barbed wire, I realised we were not going for an exchange as I had hoped. Now I understood what the two soldiers had been talking about when they said that the Lieutenant-Colonel would not take anyone in before being given a medical check-up. The camp doctor, one of several as I was soon to learn, was himself an inmate — and this man had been brought here just for this quick round of 'turn around and get out'.

All personal documents had been taken from us. Once more we were told, 'Once you are released, you'll get them back.'

I also had to leave the house keys which I had carried with me all the time. I had wanted to have them purely as a memory of our home. Hand creams which had helped me keep my problematic skin under control in Omarska were taken away from me, too. The guards asked me what they were, and I explained to the doctor the nature of my disease and how indispensable they were to me.

'You are not allowed to take any substance inside that might be harmful to your health. We will keep them in here for you, and when you need them, tell the camp doctor and he will give them to you.'

Harmful to my health? I needed them for my health. This was the same as not being allowed to open the window in Omarska because we may commit suicide — or their attack being a 'defence' to prevent us from killing their children.

A couple of weeks later, when my skin worsened, I asked the doctor for my creams. Later that day, he came back and said: 'I checked with them, and they don't remember any creams.'

While waiting again on the grass, one of the guards approached us saying he had heard that somebody amongst us had a pack of Marlboro cigarettes. A young boy from Brdo admitted he was the one. How he had managed to get these cigarettes I could not imagine. He gave the pack to the guard.

'Can you believe this?' the guard said. 'I haven't seen good cigarettes for twelve months, and while I was smoking this junk this boy smoked Marlboro.' He was overwhelmed, with a huge grin on his face. He threw his Morava cigarettes to the boy and left.

We were ordered to stand up and move further along the road. Without my belt, to which I had added five more holes, I could no longer keep my trousers on. Improvising, I kept rolling up the waist. This tightened them around the crotch, but I still had to hold them with my left hand while carrying a blanket and a bag in the right one. I dragged my feet — both from total exhaustion and because there were no shoelaces. All my energy was gone. Only sheer willpower made me move behind those before me.

A couple of days later, we were weighed and I had shrunk to just fifty-two kilograms. My normal weight had been seventy kilograms. Kasim, who had weighed over ninety kilograms before incarceration, was down to fifty-eight.

Opposite the gates of Camp One, which held two thousand civilians from Doboj, Sanski Most and Kljuc, several of those moving ahead of us were lined up — leaning against a long, concrete wall. With their hands on the wall and their legs spread apart, they were quietly answering some questions asked by the guards standing behind them. The guards were their Serb neighbours, who recognised them and singled them out for personal questioning and molesting. After each reply, they were hit with rifle butts. I could hear them groan, but they did not dare scream.

Passing these poor guys, we then stopped at the gates of

Camp Two. More than a thousand men who had entered Camp Two before us were in a hurry, trying to settle inside two cowsheds assigned to the men from Omarska. It was already approaching 5.00pm. A whole day had been required to get us inside the wire. There was no space left in the first two sheds. The guards directed us towards the last one — lying down the slope.

This shed, or the 'pavilion', as the camp authorities insisted on it being called, was my new prison. It was a long building made of large, concrete blocks — without doors or windows. Ironically, some of the men inside the camp were former employees of the company, GRO Tempo-Zagreb, that had built these sheds for the needs of JNA (Yugoslav People's Army).

The whole complex had been a JNA farm, containing nine huge cowsheds in which cattle, sheep and horses had been held. The first three sheds constituted Camp One, surrounded by barbed wire. The second three were Camp Two — also surrounded by barbed wire. The remaining three sheds still contained sheep, cattle, and horses, and were outside the camp. Camp One and Camp Two were surrounded by another ring of barbed wire, mined, and constantly guarded by armed soldiers accompanied by army dogs. Circles of wire around Camp One and Camp Two had also been mined. Close to the entrance of Camp One, there was a watch tower covering the entire area. Small wooden signs saying *mines* hung on the wires. After several heavy summer rains had washed away some of the soil, the star-shaped tops of the mines had become visible. Most people believed they were fakes.

At some later point, people started hanging their washing on the barbed wire surrounding the camp — which involved walking inside the mined area. For five or six weeks, nothing happened. Then, a newly arrived man from Kotor Varos had his leg blown off. There was a loud explosion. Stones and lumps of soil were flying about. Doctor Kusuran was running through the minefield towards the victim, who was crying for help. One boot and parts of the leg landed on the roof of the far shed. A part of the leg below the knee was missing. The man was quickly transported to a hospital in Banja Luka. We now had proof that the mines were real, but this had been knowledge acquired at a very high price.

Inside each shed, there were three separate sections. The left and the right sections where the cattle had been kept were covered with gravel. The middle section was a concrete surface — sloping from the middle in both directions. I was placed on the middle section and had to sleep on the slope, head down. We could have reversed the position, but sleeping with our heads down had been ordered by the camp authorities. Only now did I realise the use to which the ferns carried by those young men were being put. The fern-carriers were fellow inmates from the Camp One working unit, and they had also brought some straw which, together with the ferns, was used to cover the gravel and concrete and was to serve as our bedding. Chaos ensued as some inmates started to panic, fearing that they would be left without any bedding. People were actually stealing straw and ferns from each other.

Each camp had a 'Captain' — an inmate responsible for our conduct inside the wire. Their task was to implement the camp rules. In my camp, the 'Captain' was a civil engineer from Sanski Most, Muhamed Boskovic. His deputy, Sarajlic, was also from Sanski Most. Moving down the hierarchy, each shed also had its own kapo — with deputies for each of the three sections. Each section had two rows, and each row was supervised by a helper. After some weeks, the 'Captain', the kapos, their deputies and the helpers formed — together with the cooks — the camp Mafia.

Kasim entered the camp before me. He was put into the same shed — but because there were almost nine hundred men inside, it was not so easy to spot him. He was looking for me, too. When we finally spotted each other, we stayed together again. The sheds resembled large, open cans of carefully assembled human sardines.

On this first day, no food was provided. I just wanted to lie down and rest. We were again given half a mug of water each.

The next morning, the weather was beautiful. The rising of the sun was accompanied by a fresh mountain breeze. I tried to inhale enough of this clean and fresh air to make up for all the time I had missed it during the imprisonment at Omarska. The mountain was beautiful.

The breakfast, after Omarska, seemed delicious. A cup of tea — even though it was only hot water mixed with red tea powder and no sugar — a slice of brown bread, and a small piece of corned pork from a can. We did not have to run to the kitchen the way we had done in Omarska. The time set aside for eating was much longer. This was what made this breakfast so nice. Also, I could eat without fearing for my safety. I could see there was no longer any direct threat to my life.

Older Manjaca prisoners informed us that we would soon be visited and registered by the International Committee of the Red Cross (ICRC), who had been regular camp visitors for some time. This meant that the world could no longer deny our existence. We could not 'disappear' without trace any more.

Surprisingly, we discovered that a second meal was to be served, too. Lunch! We had bean soup as the camp commander, Bozidar Popovic, had said we would the day before. Portions of food were bigger than they had been in Omarska, but still not enough to replenish our starving bodies. Nevertheless, I was encouraged by these first signs of improvement. The older Manjaca prisoners told us that this improvement had begun with our arrival. Before, they had had two meals per day, but it was only soup and it was more like kitchen slops. However, when they described it, it still sounded much better than the soup in Omarska.

The food was inviting, but I could not put a spoon into my swollen mouth. My gums were virtually falling apart. A young teenager from Sanski Most working in the kitchen brought me a smaller spoon.

'Don't hurry with eating,' he said, 'take as much time as necessary to eat it properly.'

Beans served for lunch were made with animal fat — which proved too much for a stomach that had forgotten the taste of food made with anything containing fat. The following night a lot of us came down with diarrhoea, which developed into dysentery. I had stomach cramps, cold shivers and a rising body temperature. Each shed was provided with half a metal drum serving as a night toilet. When I reached the night toilet, it was already occupied by three people. I had to go to the other end of the shed and use the floor. I found more people there.

In the morning, to prevent an epidemic, we were isolated from the rest of the inmates. A small area around the shed gates was emptied just for us. We received four pills for diarrhoea each and were prescribed more hot tea. Doctor Kusuran's advice was to eat just bread and tea. The first couple of days, I had to go to the latrine up to thirty times a day until there was nothing left to pass but some strange liquid and blood. To maintain some illusion of hygiene, I made a sort of a nappy out of a piece of cloth and a plastic bag I had found as a safeguard against accidents. There were no washing facilities — only a bucket of chloride solution hanging on one of the posts.

During my illness, an army vehicle was brought inside the camp. Lorry drivers quickly installed field showers and ordered us to shower in groups of fifteen. Here was my chance to wash properly. But my hope was crushed when three soaps were cut into eight pieces each — and 1,300 people were supposed to wash with these. It was just another farce. Three soaps, one tank of water, and thirteen hundred people. Dirt had won again. After the second group, there was no soap left.

When I undressed, Kasim was astonished by the spectacle of a skeleton sitting before him. When I sat on the bench, I had a nasty shock. There was a knock when the bones hit the wood. I became really scared. I was a sitting skeleton. One of my first thoughts was of the guy who never left the infirmary. He weighed only twenty-nine kilograms. He could not walk, and from time to time, other inmates took him out and washed him. He would lie on the grass, always in the same position, feeling the sun's warmth. He was more dead than alive.

I tried to listen to the doctor's advice. I bartered my soup for bread. Kasim would also give me some bread saved from his ration. Strangely enough, underfed, exhausted, and emaciated as I was, it never occurred to me that I might easily die. I ended up with a feeling that I had no chance of recovery unless I ate my soup. I resumed eating everything I received for lunch. Sometimes, I was so weak that I could not make it to the kitchen, and one of the shed helpers would bring my portion to me. As tea was distributed from containers, and there were only a few mugs, we had to drink fast. I could not do this, so I would give the rest of my tea to Kasim. Gradually, I recovered.

Some inmates, believing they would get better food, decided to join the 'dysentery club' and to fake the illness. This had some serious implications, as Doctor Kusuran was giving them pills for diarrhoea, too. As the medication was scarce, eventually those of us who were really suffering were forced to exchange the bread rations for the necessary pills. On realising that our food was worse than theirs, these new 'patients' became miraculously cured after just two or three days. Those who wanted more tea played sick to the end.

18

A few days after our transfer from Omarska, late in the afternoon, our shed kapo, Enes Kadiric, suddenly issued a loud command.

'Stand up! Attention!'

We all got up and stood with bowed heads and hands clasped behind our backs. A figure dressed in a civilian suit entered, followed by a group of guards.

'Sit down!' The shed kapo was spitting out his lungs, trying to impress our 'guest' with his commanding abilities.

It was Vojo Kupresanin, a big political cheese in the region. Our guest, or perhaps it would be more appropriate to call him the host, delivered a speech full of 'promises'. He came to give us warm words of welcome. He came to tell us how much he cared for our welfare. He wanted to make sure that we were taken care of 'properly'.

'I am going to bring you a delegation of the ICRC to register you all as prisoners of war. You will be entitled to receive regular news bulletins.' I liked the '*I*'. Suddenly, there was rapturous applause.

'Thank you,' everybody shouted. I was surprised. It was a speech delivered by the enemy. The same man who had sent the special police squad to train the guards in Omarska in the art of killing. I was also surprised they had enough energy left to clap so loud.

Soon after, Captain Boskovic came to the shed and explained that such behaviour was most inappropriate. He strongly advised everybody not to repeat this foolish performance.

Just as the big cheese, Kupresanin, had 'promised', we finally registered with the ICRC. The registration cards held our personal details, and the date and the place of our detention. Even though we were registered as prisoners of war, which was a lie, it did not much matter to me. What mattered was that I became — at least partially — a living creature once again. I had a name. True, I was described as a prisoner of war, which was false, but what was important was that I again existed. I was alive. For two-and-a-half months, I had not existed. I could still be humiliated, but could not be ignored any longer. I was not nothing after all. I became a human being again.

Each shed had a separate ledger containing details of its inmates. The ledger helped both the ICRC and the camp officials to keep accurate records of the number of people detained. Every evening, before closing the camp gates, the deputies had to count the inmates inside their sheds and report their numbers to Captain Boskovic. He then submitted this information to the guards, who matched it against the figures from the ledgers — checking whether anyone was missing from the camp.

The ICRC members were like beings from another planet. Strange creatures dressed in nice, clean clothes. I had forgotten the way decent humans looked. I asked myself: 'What do we look like in their eyes at this moment? What do they think of us in our dirty rags, filthy, unshaven and unwashed?' Another strange thing about them was that they came to the camp, and then they left. They were free. Freedom was a thing I had almost forgotten about. It made me feel bitter. I had not done anything to deserve being incarcerated here. But nevertheless, I was also glad of their presence.

They also distributed a pack of cigarettes to each prisoner regardless of whether he was a smoker or not. They were to visit us regularly every two weeks. Probably shocked by our poor physical condition, they made a decision to break the rule of not supplying food to the camp. In addition to this extra food, some vitamins and minerals in the form of pills and tablets were provided in the hope that they would bring us back some fitness. We were also given message forms with which to contact our families in the outside world. The problem was that most of us did not know where they were or whether they were still alive. Nevertheless, and despite the fact that the camp authorities censored each message before it left the camp (we were allowed up to twenty-five words per message and no descriptions), it felt good.

I sent a message to my elder brother in Zagreb. I told him that Kasim and I were alive, and asked if he had any news about Mama. Not a single day went by without my thinking of her. I was in constant pain and fear that she must be greatly suffering from her illness if she was alive. She was a fighter, and her strong belief in God could give her enough strength to carry on. But it was difficult to fight when you were ill and lacked food and proper medical attention. Her poor health was the worst fear I had inside the camp. Still, I neither wanted to, nor could, think of the worst.

Replies started to arrive. They came not only from Bosnia and former Yugoslavia, but from all over Europe. Kasim and I received a message from our cousin Hiko from the Trnopolje camp. A hundred and forty inmates had been transferred to Trnopolje, and he wrote:

> *I was told here by those who recently arrived from Manjaca that you are being held there.*

But he said nothing about Mama. I sent our reply to Trnopolje, but before it reached him, Hiko was free. He had already left in a convoy organised by the ICRC. I was happy that at least one of our family had survived. Some weeks later, we got a reply from Zagreb.

> *Hello, Brother. Our old man and I are all right. Mother arrived and is here with us in Zagreb. She is all right.*
> *Many greetings from us.*

All my worries about Mama ceased. She had won her battle. Once I was free, she told me she had managed to obtain a little food for each day she travelled through Bosnia.

A message addressed to Senad, who was killed in Omarska when Goran Gruban had pulled the trigger too far, also arrived.

> *Dear Senad,*
> *Mother, Said, and I are all together and well. We are staying in Zagreb waiting for you to be released so that we can all together go to some third country.*

In that moment I realised that nobody had ever told Refik, Senad's father, what had happened that summer's afternoon — when he did not realise that it was his son who had been killed a short distance from where he was sitting. Nobody had had the guts to say anything as it would break this man's heart. After all, he had lost another son just a couple of years earlier. Refik was transferred to Trnopolje on the day we were sent to Manjaca. It was heartbreaking. This old man still had faith in this life. After our release in December that year, I heard Senad's younger brother went back to Bosnia to avenge his brother's death.

The presence of the ICRC members provided benefits in many different ways. They did not just ensure that no inmate 'disappeared' without a trace, but also, apart from medicine and food, they supplied us with warm, dark horse blankets which helped in the harsh mountain winter conditions. At the approach of winter, we all received a pack containing warm underwear and a woollen cap. The underwear labels showed it had been bought in Croatia, but when the ICRC decided to supply each one of us with a pair of shoes, the Chetniks demanded that these be bought from their supplier in Banja Luka. The ICRC had no choice but to buy them there or to leave us without shoes. They also had to pay inflated prices. Before their distribution, many inmates — Kasim amongst them — had only slippers, real or improvised.

When our release before the new year became less certain, the ICRC had to pay the Serbs around fifty thousand German marks to provide the sheds with heating. The 'stoves' were halved oil drums welded on top, costing no more than twenty marks each. Even if they had been proper stoves, there was no way the sheds could be heated. There were numerous openings in the walls and the roof. I supposed the ICRC allowed this blackmail, knowing it was helping them in their negotiations for our release. On the other hand, I was afraid of negative consequences, as the Serbs could see our detention as a ready source of money.

The ICRC was also providing money for wood used in the kitchen — including for fuel for its delivery from the forest — and for the transportation of water. For about two months, lorries did supply the camp with decent drinking water. Then it was stopped. The transportation fuel was redirected for the forced labour in the nearby forest. Instead, we were given a great number of plastic canisters, once more provided by the ICRC, in which to bring water each day from the nearby pond.

Half of the food provided for us by the ICRC was unloaded straight away at Serb barracks, some three kilometres further from the camp. The ICRC had to pay this price in order to be allowed to bring us any food. More of our food supplies were stored in one of the bungalows at the camp entrance. The supplies unused by the time of the next ICRC visit were quickly moved to the camp kitchens.

The Chetniks always liked to put their hands into somebody else's belongings. Not even the camp commander could suppress his instincts. Cursing us for receiving 'such good food', he would regularly put his hand in the boxes being carried from the ICRC lorries to the kitchens — taking out a pack of biscuits or a can of meat. Later on, when the ICRC managed to successfully negotiate the delivery of packages sent by families, these were thoroughly searched by the guards for cigarettes and biscuits.

'Fuck the meat,' they said. 'We've got plenty of it. We want biscuits and foreign cigarettes.'

Apart from the ICRC delegation, we had other visitors, too. Most of the time, they were reporters from the western world. It was they who raised public awareness in the West about 'ethnic cleansing' in the region. A delegation of European Community observers, led by Colm Doyle, tried to get more information. They wanted to know the places we had come from, what happened there, whether we were soldiers or ordinary civilians, whether we had fought or not, and so on. They seemed to be trying to establish a clearer picture of events, which must have been presented by the Serbs in a totally different light. Each time the Serbs talked to the media, or to any other visitors, we were presented as brutal combatants who had intended to commit genocide against their people. We heard the camp commander describing us in this way, but of course, we could not protest. Some more enthusiastic inmates tried to communicate with the European Community observers. Some spoke fluent French. Others, using a few words of English or German, asked about the possibility of the camp closing, and of our release.

None of these visits excited me a great deal. I did not believe they would bring about any significant change. They never brought any news of negotiations for our release. I saw the French cabinet minister, Bernard Kouchner, as no more than a tourist to whom we were rarities not seen on European soil since World War II.

Deep down, I was preparing myself for a lengthy stay here. I believed we would have to wait for the conflict to finish before we could expect release — if we lived that long. And I believed the conflict would last for years. I knew it was virtually impossible to survive winter in this place. In this mountain territory, in winter, temperatures reached minus twenty degrees centigrade and trees broke under the weight of the snow. I struggled to believe that I would not fall victim to the winter.

19

Those who had only ever been incarcerated in Manjaca had had their hair shaved off as a prevention against the spread of lice. We had brought our lice from Omarska with us, and it was time to have our heads shorn. The camp authorities issued an order that everyone must have his head shaved. Two barbers managed to deal with some fifty heads per day. But the camp regularly suffered from power cuts. Inmates were returning to the sheds with some unconventional hair styles. Some had the top of their head shaved bald — but with hair sticking out on both sides. Some had one side shaved completely bald, and the other still untouched. It was the time of new trends in hair-styling for us inmates, and the reason for these new looks was the power failure which had occurred in the middle of the shaving.

The barbers were outside our barbed wire, and in my case my fear from Omarska returned. I only felt safe at Manjaca when I was inside the wire, and for a long time I was very reluctant to go beyond it. Once again, I waited to go to the only known open-air 'salon' in the Balkans with the last group of customers. I was shorn in seconds. The hairless style preferred by our captors made us all have a good laugh.

The very hot August weather was unbearable inside the shed, but we were not permitted to leave it. Only small groups of twenty to thirty were allowed to spend a short time, usually half an hour, on the slope above the shed. Visits to and from different sheds were subject to very tough restrictions, which prevented brothers separated inside the camp from seeing each other.

Lying on the ground next to the shed doors, I watched flocks of swallows flying around in their thousands. I admired them for their flying, their ability to rise above the camp, above the wire that encircled us. I admired them for being able to sense when it was time to fly south at the approach of cold weather. From time to time, they were scared off by a loony pilot. A low flying jet fighter would pierce the air above the shed, which shook under the huge pressure created by the plane.

The brutality of the camp beatings was far less severe than it had been in Omarska. There were no killings. Fear of death receded. Death at the hands of our captors no longer followed us at every step. It was not lurking behind every corner. People relaxed and gradually became themselves again. The camp regime relaxed, too — or rather, we relaxed the regime ourselves. Some inmates started breaking camp rules, knowing they would not be punished by execution. Soon after, others began to follow their example — until finally everyone started coming out of the sheds. This would provoke the guards, who would shout at us to return inside. Eventually, they would storm inside the wire and, hitting everybody at random, they would herd us back inside the buildings. Occasionally, there were more serious incidents, such as when the inmates from Camp One refused to go to work. The guards ran inside the camp armed with shovels, and two inmates ended up with broken limbs.

Being confined to the sheds and without fear of death, people occupied themselves with various activities. Some were still writing recipes they had started collecting in Omarska. Trading flourished. A lot of people took to wood-carving, but trading was most widespread. Clothes, shoes, watches, camp-produced cigarette holders and pipes, new shoes and soaps supplied by the ICRC, leather jackets, even food. There were customers for all this merchandise. The currency was cigarettes — supplied fortnightly by the ICRC, or smuggled inside the camp by middlemen who acted on behalf of the guards. The guards traded cigarettes for foreign currency, if available, or for new shoes, leather jackets and soaps. There were a few die-hards who still possessed some foreign currency — such as Ceric, who bought cigarettes with German marks from a camp guard through a middleman. Another guard spotted this transaction. Ceric's cigarettes and the rest of his money were confiscated. His punishment was to stand where he had been caught, immobile, head down, and hands clasped behind him, for a couple of hours.

Many pairs of new shoes ended up on the other side of the wire. People with old, but still warm shoes sold their new pair to the guards for cigarettes. Middlemen who kept this trade alive said these shoes usually ended up in private shops in Banja Luka or in the local market. Soap was cheaper. Four cigarettes flew over the wire and the deal was done. Under ICRC pressure, the camp command ordered this trade to stop at once. We were sternly forbidden to trade in shoes by a guard with a new pair of ICRC shoes on his feet.

Prices on the thriving market, which took place in front of my shed, were constantly fluctuating. The items being offered for sale, and sometimes for barter, included canned fish, bread rations, and packs of biscuits. Clothes, shoes, and cigarette holders did not appear on the market. These were circulated from shed to shed.

Supply and demand dictated prices. Most often, suppliers were smokers and buyers non-smokers. When new food arrived in the camp, supply exceeded demand and the prices went down. As the time went on, there was less and less food on the market and consequently the prices went up. The food supply was at its lowest and the prices at their highest a few days before the next visit by the ICRC.

A variety of different characters surfaced. Some always wanted to be freshly shaven and wear clean clothes as much as conditions would allow. They used cigarettes to buy clothes brought to the camp in family packets delivered by the ICRC. Smoking addicts sold everything for another cigarette, even their bread rations. If they could, as the saying goes in Bosnia, they would sell their legs beneath them for a cigarette. In periods when they had neither cigarettes nor anything to sell, they smoked dried ferns wrapped in paper from cement sacks.

Non-smokers only thought about how to buy more food. The lords of the camp were the cooks and their friends. They always had enough to eat. They had surplus food, and they never bothered to come to the market. Word of mouth about extra supplies would bring happy eaters to their door.

Gamblers had no concern for profit. They would win or lose everything simply for the love of gambling, or to escape the reality. When they lost everything, they went to work in the forest.

Kasim and I rarely got involved in trade. We ate any food we received. Once we bartered chocolate for two cans of mackerel. We 'bought' the fish from some friends of the cooks who never went hungry, and just wanted to indulge in eating chocolate. A block of chocolate cost ten cigarettes in the market place. Kasim, Himzo and I shared the cigarettes we received.

In this process of buying and selling, no one could be cheated easily. Buyers would go around assessing the size of each piece of bread — and its freshness and softness — before making their final decision. The normal price for a quarter of bread was three or four cigarettes in the height of the season. When necessary, rabid smokers would sell such a piece of bread for two cigarettes. Cans of fish were always the same. They could not be haggled over for size, freshness or softness — so their price never varied much. Smokers would sometimes lower the price to one cigarette less than their competitors, and here speed and luck were necessary.

The distribution of cigarettes would enliven everyone. Gambling took place all day and night. In the dark, improvised oil lamps were used to provide the light for the game, which was observed by many of those not taking part in it. Himzo and I once took part in a game of poker, despite Kasim's prediction that we would lose. We lost a whole pack — twenty cigarettes gone. It was the equivalent of ten cans of smoked sardines or almost two fresh loaves of bread. Crni, on the other hand, was a child of fortune for more than a week. He won of a number of poker games, acquiring a staggering seven packs of cigarettes. He was rich. He could afford special treats on the market — powdered milk and cocoa powder, which could be mixed with a bit of water to create a special spread for the bread. He was our neighbour and he was generous. He shared his cigarettes and special treats with us. The trouble was that he could not stop gambling. Gambling helped him to switch off from his surroundings. So, he would lose it all again. One day, he brought seven packs of cigarettes and asked me to keep them for him. 'And no matter what happens, don't give them back to me,' he said.

Soon after, Ibrahim came to me and said smiling: 'Crni wants his cigarettes back.'

'No,' I said. 'Go back and tell him I'm not here.'

Expecting Crni to come for the cigarettes in person, I left the shed and hid behind it. Ibrahim found me again.

'He's not going to stop.'

'Did you tell him you couldn't find me?'

'He didn't believe me.'

Later, I saw Crni coming with his hands in his trouser pockets. He was smiling.

'Easy come, easy go,' his smile said. He sat down with us, and we shared a cigarette he had given us earlier as a present. He was still a winner. He had had a good time. Having no more chips for gambling, he decided to go and work in the forest for a change. He was the champion of the camp days at Manjaca. He always helped whenever he could, and he never did any harm to anyone.

One day, somebody came up with the idea of running a bingo game. It was the most profitable operation in the camp. Most of us were trying to buy our luck with one cigarette — the prize being twenty cigarettes. The winner always looked happy, but the organiser pocketed five times more.

Wood-carving, which had started as a means of breaking the boredom, soon became a business. Most of the artisans made nicely-carved wooden pipes and cigarette holders, even though they had never made such things before. It turned out that there were quite a few artists around who had not known before that they had the skill in them.

This artistry and business grew out of necessity. Without a cigarette holder, the end of the cigarette would be wasted, as it would burn the fingers and lips. Holders were needed, and there were none to be found. It was exciting to see people creating something from nothing. They did not even have the necessary tools, but this did not seem to bother them. They would steal a spoon from the kitchen (there were no forks or knives), and they would make a knife out of the spoon handle — hammering it with a stone to create a rough blade. This was then further sharpened on the pipes in the shed. These DIY knives served not only as tools for carving wood, but also as effective can openers — fish cans were often supplied without the openers. Some made proper handles for their knives, others just wrapped the end in a piece of cloth.

The knife itself was not enough, though. The most important tool of the carving kit was a drill. They were fragile, more like surgical instruments than carving tools. They required gentle handling because they broke easily. Ekro was one of the few proud owners of a drill. He was handy with anything. You named it, he made it for you. I watched his incredible hands turning a piece of wire into a perfect drill. He had large hands, used to rough, hard work. It seemed impossible that such hands could perform any kind of delicate operation — but he had a fine, sensitive touch and he worked with incredible precision.

Beech wood was most often used for the carving. It was obtainable from the kitchen. However, maple was softer and easier to carve and drill. Several young maple trees around the camp lost half of their branches as a result. When this hobby turned into a profitable business, cigarette holders and pipes became works of art. The artists experimented with different kinds of wood. The most highly prized were small pieces of red plum and cherry wood. To the delight of the camp artists, these were supplied — together with walnut — by the camp's labour force working in the forest.

Once the carving of a cigarette holder was finished, a tiny piece of fish-can was inserted into the opening that held the cigarette to prevent the wood from burning. At this stage, the rough work was done. Then, the final touches that gave the holder a feeling of smoothness were done with small pieces of bottle-glass, which could be found all over the place. Those who risked smuggling sand paper and lacquer from the workshop made their products even more glossy.

The champion of all the artists was a man in his thirties from Sanski Most. His work included a whole plethora of designs. He had a box in which he kept some thirty differently designed holders. These were for sale. For his own pleasure, he carved larger holders celebrating the beauty of women, which looked like the Three Graces on Botticelli's Primavera. These were not for sale.

When the Chetniks in the forest spotted the cigarette holders used by the camp workforce, they wanted them, too. Through this channel, the cigarette-holder business spread outside the camp wire. Depending on the quality, the Chetniks were prepared to pay a price between seven and twenty cigarettes. One of the Chetniks was admiring his holder — turning it around, obviously delighting in it, when he said: 'These people are incredible. If we gave them all the necessary equipment, in two weeks, they would push a plane out of their shed.'

The carving business diversified. A small piece of flat wood was decorated with various symbols, most commonly name initials. It was usually worn as a pendant hanging on a piece of thread around the neck. If you wanted to have an inscription by the most talented hand around, you went to Ismet. Some twenty years earlier, he had produced counterfeit banknotes that even experts could not differentiate from the real ones. For this display of skill, he had served a good number of years in an institution for rehabilitation — a communist euphemism for prison. He had landed there not through his inability to deceive the experts, but through betrayal by his partner.

When somebody mentioned that an inmate from Sanski Most, a tailor by profession, had made the first pair of trousers inside the camp, Ekro said: 'So what! I can do it, too. He makes them for twenty cigarettes and I'll make a pair for half that price.' Everybody looked at him with suspicion, but no one commented. Using an ICRC blanket, the little devil actually did it. They were not as straight as could be wished, but they served the purpose.

Refik Sisic, a well-known hairdresser from Prijedor, volunteered in the camp to perform the duty of my shed's barber. This usually involved shaving the whole lot, usually some nine hundred beards and moustaches — not counting several of those who were young and still beardless — using four razors supplied by the camp authorities every four weeks or so. To do this so gently that you did not feel your beard hairs pulled out by force was a real art. But then Mister Sisic, as he was called by everyone, was nothing less than an artist. He was not a typical hairstylist, boring you to death with stories and questions you were not interested in answering. He did this job to pass his time, but also to help us. Unlike some other 'barbers' (these guys cashed in on those who wanted to be shaved more often than every two weeks by Mister Sisic), he did not ask to be paid for his service. He would shave you while whistling some old tune, and the only question would be: 'Is it painful?' If there has ever been a barber angel it must be Mister Sisic.

Mister Sisic, Sero Velic from my village, and Suad Hadzic, a former manager at Celpak, Prijedor's paper-producing factory, made a chess set working as a team. They carefully carved all thirty-two pieces. When all the pieces were finally lined on the board made of cardboard, they looked magnificent. From that time on, this board was a battlefield on which Sisic, Sero, Hodza, Crni and others gave their all to beat each other.

Manjaca also served as a labour camp. Before my transfer, inmates from Sanski Most and Kljuc, who had been there for two-and-a-half months, had carried out huge amounts of work. Every morning, they were taken out of the camp to dig trenches, or to build a water supply system nearby. For this they were given more food — usually half a loaf of bread supplemented with wild fruit they had picked in the breaks between work. They tried to smuggle the fruit to their friends and later, when cigarettes entered the camp as currency, they would sell it. Once the camp guards discovered this activity, they banned it immediately. Each member of the workforce had to empty his pockets on entering the camp.

Several inmates from Doboj were formed into a working unit operating inside the camp. Their task was to look after the cattle and sheep brought from our deserted villages. The animals were kept in the three remaining sheds behind Camp Two. The working unit also did repairs to maize barns, and prepared cattle feed. Moving around the camp freely, they had access to fruit trees dispersed throughout the camp. For months, I heard fabulous stories about their menu. Milking the cows provided them with a chance to produce thick sour cream, cottage cheese, and yoghurt, which when combined with maize polenta made a delicious meal. Being in constant touch with the camp guards, some of them also worked as middlemen in sales transactions across the wire. These few, lucky men were beneficiaries of their work in many ways.

Perhaps the most difficult work was in the forest, where day in and day out, in the sun and in the rain, several hundred men (including volunteers) chopped and transported wood for up to eight hours a day. They left the camp even before breakfast was finished, and were back inside the wire late in the evening. Some felled trees, while others carried the heavy tree trunks on their shoulders up steep, slippery paths where mountain goats would fear to tread. The guards and the frontline fighters on leave were entitled to sell these tree trunks for firewood in lieu of pay.

Each morning, the camp command demanded a number of workers from a different shed — but most of the time the working unit was a mixture of volunteers from all sheds. The reasons behind this readiness for work were food and cigarettes. As an incentive to work harder, the Chetniks would give each forest worker five cigarettes per day.

Once they were back in the shed, they proudly displayed the cigarettes earned.

'There was also plenty of food,' they would say. 'Half a loaf and two bowls of thick potato soup.'

The very words brought broad smiles to their faces. But there was exhaustion in their eyes. I admired them, but at the same time I felt sorry for them because they suffered greatly during their work. How long could they last this way? This was not a question they asked themselves. Their determination to turn their bad situation into a better one was manifested in the only way they knew — through hard work and disregard for the pain.

I always tried to avoid doing any kind of work. I was neither keen to better my situation through hard work, nor was I willing to work for the Chetniks. The last thing I was prepared to do was to allow them to benefit from my effort. If these guys had not volunteered for work, I might have ended up working for the enemy. I used my skin problem as an excuse not to work. During morning roll-call, I would hide in another shed — or I would spend this time in the latrine faking stomach problems. Doctor Kusuran finally gave me a piece of paper which I could effectively use to fend off that bastard, Alisic, the shed deputy, who insisted that my skin was *my* problem.

Probably the best job in the camp was the workshop close to the camp command. This small hut employed the skills of wood-carvers. Their carvings ended up as souvenirs in the houses of the camp officials. The workshop craftsmen ranged from self-taught inmates who had never done this kind of work before, to members of the Bosnia–Herzegovina Arts Academy. Next to their hut, some others worked as camp mechanics, servicing army vehicles and farming machinery. In the autumn, two brothers from the latter group were chosen to plough the farmland around the camp.

Short work on road repairs took place in the summer, and at approximately the same time, the Chetniks decided to realise their dream of having a church built by the Muslims. Construction workers, helped by those with no similar skills, built the church near the camp pond — which took them several months. This was why the cement I saw stored in a bungalow on my arrival had been needed. Day after day, the new construction rose higher and higher. The church roof was made of copper, collected from the domes of dynamited mosques in the Sanski Most–Kljuc region.

Not every Chetnik was delighted with the new building.

'Fuck the church built by *Balije*,' was Spaga's short comment.

The camp commander, Bozidar Popovic, had a lot of leisure time on his hands. He planned his second retirement once the camp closed. The man's long-lasting dream was to be a sailor. Why not use this free labour to put his master plan into effect?

Several inmates were chosen to build a small boat. The boat was never finished. But even if it had been finished, the camp commander lacked the most important ingredient he needed for this hobby. He needed the sea. He probably counted on his bearded brothers in Kninska Krajina to get him a part of the Croatian coast by the end of the summer. He rubbed his palms, saying into his chin: 'It'll happen soon. You'll get your sea.'

But the summer passed, the boat remained unfinished, and the sea seemed to be as far away as ever. Well, who knows? In some other life, he may complete the boat, and maybe even catch a big swordfish.

20

Bosnia was further divided within the camp as regional divisions developed. The cooks, who were all from Sanski Most, were giving more food to 'their' people from their town — which we from the Kozarac–Prijedor region resented.

By cutting down our rations, they created a surplus which was then sold for cigarettes. Additional rations, out of this surplus, could be bought for two cigarettes. Similarly, they created a surplus of bread rations. A quarter of a loaf — two cigarettes; half a loaf — four cigarettes. When fresh bread arrived, the kitchen staff were selling it via their accomplices outside the kitchen at ten to twelve cigarettes a loaf. They never tried to keep it secret. They handled the food as if it were their own property.

The kitchen staff numbered ten to fifteen men. Some had had previous experience in catering, but most had had nothing to do with cooking whatsoever. They, of course, ate better than the rest of us. They cooked their food in a separate, large pot. Once I was given lunch from their pot by a camp doctor, and it was real food.

The inmates from Sanski Most never complained, and their plates were regularly topped. They never had to buy additional food. When we complained, it was threatened that we would be reported to the camp authorities. 'For whatever excuse we come up with' — these were their very words. A report of this kind meant a week spent in a solitary cell, seasoned with beatings. We persisted nevertheless, and the upshot was that a couple of men from Prijedor were included in the kitchen team. This brought no improvement, as 'our' men made no attempt to introduce any changes.

The kitchen staff had the full support of the camp kapos. My shed kapo was Enes Kadiric, and his deputies were Sabahudin Alisic, Edin Mrkalj and Ceric. They all knew each other. Kadiric was from Brdo, and the others from Ljubija, a small town next to it. Kadiric and Mrkalj performed this duty from the beginning, and after removing deputies from Kozarac — which was a sort of a camp coup — they had installed Alisic (cousin of Kadiric) and Ceric instead. They had taken full control of the shed. But when some inmates tried to steal food or eat twice, they did not hesitate to report them. I had to ask myself often: 'Whose side are they on? Are they aware of the consequences of their actions? Do they realise that they are putting the lives of these people at risk?'

It was a master–servant situation. When the Chetniks shouted, they jumped. When they shouted, they expected us to jump. Fortunately, Boskovic, the inmate appointed head of Camp Two, was a wise man. He always tried to deal with problems inside the wire without involving the Chetniks. When one inmate was caught cheating, trying to obtain double rations for his lunch, Boskovic prevented his subordinates reporting the incident and advised the inmate not to repeat the same mistake again. Nevertheless, Alisic and Kadiric retained this inmate's ICRC identification card, which served as a pass to the kitchen, and they let him go hungry for two days. This was in direct violation of the ICRC rules, which stated that the card could be kept by no one but the designated holder.

Every few weeks, the camp authorities would deliver some three hundred kilograms of beef that came from our slaughtered cows. An isolated small piece of this meat would occasionally be found here and there in our soup. The kapos and the cooks on the other hand had a feast. They even competed with each other as to who could make the biggest steak in the shortest possible time. There was a hierarchy in the kitchen, too. And only those at the top of the kitchen ladder could participate in these competitions.

While they enjoyed regular feasts, we combated hunger in many different ways. True, the food we received here was more than in Omarska, but it was not enough. Those who worked received more food. I was not prepared to work, so I thought about food all the time — which in turn made me feel hungry all the time.

In front of the gates of Camp Two stood a pile of dried maize. It was animal feed. On our way back from the pond, I would steal one or two ears. So did many others. It was very dry, hard, and tough to chew. I remembered that even our animals had trouble chewing them. I needed not only strong teeth, but also strong nerves. Little by little, I learned how to soften them with saliva — enough to make the kernels give up the struggle. Gradually, I progressed from only several grains to managing a whole ear. It did not taste good — as a matter of fact, it was disgusting. However, it did serve to suppress my constant thoughts about food.

Some got fed up with eating raw maize. They tried to cook it on the fire in the kitchen. But the kitchen staff would not allow it. Atko, the head of the kitchen, would swear at them — mentioning their mothers. Cursing them, he would then chuck the ears out of the fire and into the rubbish. Seeing him approaching, the owners would rush to grab their maize before he did.

Desperate smokers again did not eat the maize, but would sell it. One ear a cigarette. On one occasion, Crni gave me some baked maize. It did not taste much better than the raw stuff.

With the passing of time, I became a real expert in eating raw maize. I could eat a whole ear in ten minutes. Once I ate three ears, two of which were still fairly green. When Kasim spotted three bare cobs, he said: 'No, you didn't.'

'Yes, I did.'

He could not believe it. 'You gobbled it up faster than a donkey,' he said. I just laughed.

I started having stomach cramps. For several days, the maize fermented in my stomach and I could not get rid of it. Bourbon was maturing in the most unusual place. The pain and wind were agonising. I belched enormous amounts of stale air. I had long bouts of wind that sounded like air raid warnings. If I had been on the front line, I could have been used as a deadly weapon to neutralise the enemy forces.

A man named Bane soaked maize in an empty mackerel can filled with water. Overnight, the grains would became soft — and therefore easy to chew and digest.

Ekro would put grains in a can full of oil, and add a pinch of salt. Then he would make a fire on the walkway between our blankets and fry the maize. Everybody laughed. He sold a can of fried maize for one cigarette.

Another way of getting some food was to steal cabbage and potatoes from the kitchen. Potato and cabbage sacks stood close to the tables where we were eating. The kitchen staff always kept an eye on them, but Karaba's hands were quicker than the cooks' eyes. His speciality was cabbage. He would snatch it in a fraction of a second. He was always prepared to sell it if offered the right price. Ekro was his regular customer. Using his DIY knife, Ekro would slice the cabbage. Adding a dash of salt that he had obtained from the kitchen, he would have a perfect salad. We laughed again.

'What's so funny?' he would ask. 'It's really good. Come on. Have some.' He offered some to Kasim, Himzo and me. I have to admit it was really good. He would save half of it and eat it in the kitchen with his soup.

The cooks would always throw away the cabbage core. On their way to the rubbish depot, the cores would be snatched by some inmates who always inspected the rubbish baskets. Hard, sweet cabbage roots were a real treat for them.

A few regularly searched the rubbish depot. Others would shout at them not to humiliate themselves. They would yell: 'Get out, pigs.'

Hemas once found a kilogram of good potatoes. Maybe he had a deal with somebody in the kitchen who sneaked them out for him. They were no use raw. To bake them in the kitchen was out of the question. At that time, a hole dug for a new latrine still stood empty and clean. Hemas and a friend of his lit a fire in the hole and were baking potatoes in a large empty can. The smoke attracted the attention of a passing guard. He indicated to us to keep quiet and walked towards the hole. Hemas and his friend were too preoccupied with their potatoes to notice him. The guard reached the hole and said: 'Oh, I see — a second kitchen has started work.' Everybody laughed. Hemas and his friend were confused. 'Extinguish the fire and get out of there,' the guard said. They were scared, but did not forget to take their potatoes with them.

We had some exceptionally thin people. The most famous one was Rezak Salesevic — who although he looked like a stickman had been nicknamed Rambo. For some reason, Spaga became very fond of him. He instructed the kitchen staff to let Rambo eat as much as he liked. The whole camp loved Rambo. He was a very likeable person, but Atko, the kitchen master, resented him. He refused to let Rambo have a second helping. Rambo complained to Spaga, who then introduced a new rule. If he finished his meal in time to join the next group before they entered the kitchen, Rambo was allowed to eat nine meals.

One day after breakfast, Rambo walked around crestfallen. He was normally a very cheerful person and this was out of character.

'What's the problem? What went wrong?' somebody asked him.

'I managed to eat only seven times.' The story circulated from shed to shed, and the whole camp laughed for days.

Inmates known and unknown to Rambo asked him to give them some of his extra rations, and he would share them with them. The Chetniks thought he was crazy, but he was not. He was a natural born comedian. His performances always gathered large audiences. A young Serb officer, attracted by Rambo's entertainment of a crowd, stopped and exchanged a few words with him — finally using a common Bosnian expression: 'Somebody is missing a plank in the head.'[1]

'Somebody is missing a plank, and somebody an entire saw-mill,' was Rambo's instant reply. The audience exploded with laughter, and the only person who did not get it was the young officer.

Rambo's huge appetite gave the cooks an idea to introduce a competition to find out which inmate could eat the most soup rations. The winner was E. J. While still at home, E. J. would eat a kilogram of fat bacon for breakfast. In this competition, he easily ate fourteen full plates of thick bean soup. He made a bet with the cooks that he could eat twenty loaves of bread soaked for twenty minutes in warm milk. They didn't have courage to put his claim to the test. E. J. was triumphant.

---

1. In Bosnia, 'to miss a plank in the head' means 'to have a screw loose'.

The ICRC supplied us with biscuits. Later on, they added fruit. Two tangerines and two apples fortnightly were a real treat. After 'censorship' by the camp authorities, the remaining boxes were supposed to be evenly distributed to each shed. However, the kapos and the cooks always managed to 'censor' a few more, which ended up in the kitchen. The cooks used them to make cakes for themselves and the rest of the camp's élite.

This kind of abuse took place in many different forms. At first, there was no running water, washing powder or soap. Then the ICRC distributed some washing powder — but we had to use drinking water for washing purposes. Several of us would soak our clothes in a small bucket, in the same solution of powder — which after each round was getting dirtier and dirtier. It had to be done this way, for if everybody used fresh water and fresh powder only a few of us would manage to wash the clothes. Still, this way of doing it was better than not doing it at all. Then the camp authorities discontinued the supplies of drinking water altogether, and the camp Mafia secretly 'censored' all provisions of washing powder. Each day, we had to haul water from a nearby pond. I regularly joined a group going to the pond. Water from the first round was for the kitchen, and the second round was usually for our use. Many times, we had to give up our last drops of drinking water so that the soup could be finished on time. At the same time, we would see the cooks having a hot shower and their clothes soaked in hot water and 'censored' washing powder. The soaps we collected could finally be used. The surplus was used as drinking water.

This abuse was partially corrected when the ICRC started providing everybody with a bar of soap. Kasim and I had two showers before the cold weather started, and washed our clothes one last time. These were the only showers we had had in seven months. One of us always had to squat by the wire and the small maple tree next to it — guarding our drying clothes. Leaving them unattended even for a moment meant they would get stolen. The thieves usually sold stolen clothes across the wire to the inmates from Camp One.

The kitchen staff also bought watches and jewellery. Those of us who had been at Omarska had nothing left, but those who had been at Manjaca all the time still had their valuables with them. The camp authorities knew about this trade and carefully monitored the transactions, but did not interfere. However, days before our release, Rifko and Kemo, the two main traders in valuables, were put in prison and subjected to thorough interrogation. This delighted us ordinary members of the camp. The valuables they had acquired were confiscated. We were pleased because it was unforgivable that in these inhuman conditions they would take advantage of their privileged position for personal gain — exploiting the weaknesses and the need of their fellow prisoners. What would someone do if his life depended on their help?

Some of the kitchen staff hoarded possessions away like chipmunks. During one of the routine camp searches, the guards found under Halupa's blankets some ten woolly caps, several pairs of warm underwear and ten packs of cigarettes. Why did he need all these? Was it his natural instinct, or was he damaged so much by his camp experiences that he thought he would not be able to provide himself with some clothes once he was released into the outside world?

The assumption that the treatment inside the camp might have left a deep imprint on Halupa was partially confirmed when another non-smoker, Huzeir, took his hoard of cigarettes with him to the Red Cross Reception Centre in Croatia. When Ekro asked: 'What do you need them for there? You don't smoke,' Huzeir's reply was: 'You know very well that people in Croatia smoke, too.'

I could not believe my ears. His perception of the outside world that he was about to rejoin did not differ from the world he was about to leave. I found it astonishing that he took the cigarettes with him instead of leaving them for his brother who was staying behind — and who was a smoker.

Before arriving at Manjaca, I could never have dreamt I would have so many words of criticism for my fellow inmates. We, who had been through so much, could so easily divide without any force being imposed upon us. I began to doubt the survival of Bosnia.

21

Two weeks after our arrival at Manjaca, the hundred and seventy-four inmates who had remained in Omarska arrived in two buses. Spaga then took out a list and called out a hundred and seventy names. He announced they should take their belongings and leave the shed. They were selected for a transfer to Trnopolje. We could not guess on what basis they had been chosen. They included men of all age groups. Some of those selected were in worse physical condition than others, but many who suffered severe health disorders (for example, Kevac, who still had a bullet in his leg) remained behind.

We found out why that last group had been retained in Omarska. They served two purposes. One was to show the world that Omarska was not a concentration camp, but a transit centre. The Serbs tried to convince the world that only small groups of inmates were staying at Omarska for the purpose of the investigation of 'crimes' against the Serbs — after which they would be transferred somewhere else. The other purpose was to wash off the blood stains, to sweep away the remains of hair, broken teeth, even pieces of flesh, and to destroy the personal documents of those who had seen their last light there. Bullet holes were masked in various ways. Amongst other documents of the kind, Himzo, a young man from my village, found inside the 'Red House' the personal ID and driving licence of Mirsad Klipic — a man from my village who was taken out one night by Zeljko Meakic. This was further proof that those taken out for one of many 'exchanges' never lived to be exchanged.

While doing these grisly jobs, the inmates of this last group had their food rations increased to half a loaf of bread and two meals per day for the benefit of the western journalists. They were actually forced to eat more than their shrunken stomachs could take.

To give the western journalists the impression that we had slept in some comfort, the Chetniks even brought army cots to Omarska. But the cleaning squad had to sleep underneath them on the floor. An inmate from Kozarusa, known by the nickname 'Bokser', was their kapo. He was given powers by Zeljko Meakic to keep the cleaning squad under control. He adopted Chetnik methods, ferociously beating all those who dared speak to him. He spent his time with the guards as if he were one of them.

Some three weeks after the cleaning squad (the showpiece squad) arrived at Manjaca, some of them — plus some one hundred other former Omarska inmates — gradually left the camp. The first ones to leave were young men from Jakupovici, who unfortunately ended up in Mali Logor, a military prison in Banja Luka. The others were exchanged. On the other hand, Major Mirso and Captain Cirkin, former JNA officers of Muslim nationality, were brought over from Mali Logor. Both of them had been taken out of Omarska way back on 28 May together with a group of men from my village. Kasim enquired after these men but received a most disappointing answer.

'Nobody from Kevljani was in Mali Logor with us.' This meant that our villagers, Hamed, Zido, Nijaz, Ilijaz, had 'disappeared' and there was very little hope they could be still alive. That same summer, a high-ranking Bosnian Army officer asked for his brothers, Nagib and Omer Mahmuljin, from Kozarac, to be brought to central Bosnia for an exchange. A group of Serb JNA officers came to the Manjaca camp to look for them. Both Nagib and Omer had been chosen in Omarska for 'exchange' along with many others. Some Omarska guards had spread a rumour that a certain number of detainees, amongst them Sakib Pervanic, had been selected to work on farms in Topola and Bosanska Gradiska — near the Croatian border. Having been given this information by some former Omarska inmates, these Serb officers left for Omarska and continued on to Topola and Gradiska to look for the Mahmuljin brothers. Several days later, the officers were back at Manjaca. The news they gave us was that nobody had been held at either Omarska, Gradiska or Topola at the time of their visits.

This information confirmed that none of those allegedly taken out of the camp for work or 'exchange' had actually ever ended up at Topola or Gradiska. It is certainly more realistic to assume that all of these men had been executed somewhere within or close to the vicinity of Omarska camp.

On September 15, the first group of a more significant size had been released. Sixty-nine survivors from Omarska were considered to be in urgent need of proper medical care. They were evacuated by a Russian Army plane to a hospital near London.

Even though several individuals were sent home to Prijedor and Sanski Most, it turned out not to be home any more — but a place where they never felt safe from the death squads that were now the only law in both towns.

A group of imams and teenagers met the same destiny after their transfer to the headquarters of Merhamet, a Muslim charity in Banja Luka. They were confined to Merhamet premises exclusively, because outside they would face insecurity and danger. After this, no one experienced freedom for a long, long time.

In October, the camp population increased once more. Around four hundred new civilians were brought in. They were also labelled Muslim extremists caught during the fighting. They wore civilian clothes. They were all over forty and most of them were from Kotor Varos. Some of them shared our shed. Others were from Jajce. All of a sudden, I realised that stories of Derventa, Modrica and Jajce falling into Serb hands had been true. Before this, I had refused to believe it. At the time of our incarceration in the Omarska camp, these towns were still free. I wanted to believe they were still in our hands. The fall of Jajce made me remember what the soldier on the bus during the journey from Omarska had said. Bosnia really was shrinking to the size of a *fildzan*.

At this time, all ethnic Croats were taken to be exchanged for Serb prisoners of war held by the Croats. As soon as they got on the buses, their escorts forced each one of them to swallow a handful of salt. Then they offered them water — which they quickly grabbed in the hope of extinguishing the unbearable thirst. But the water was salted, too. Again they had to sing Serb nationalistic songs, and were beaten with truncheons. When they arrived at the place of exchange, the Croats turned down the deal. They refused to exchange genuine Serb fighters with no signs of ill-treatment or malnutrition for these civilian human ruins. Part of the deal was also for a Croat officer to be exchanged who had not been brought there, and who was at that time sitting in Manjaca.

The Croats were then taken to a military compound in Knin, where they spent the night. Anybody passing by the compound was allowed to have a go at beating them. Army irregulars, police, women, even children, vented their anger on these exhausted men. Bruised and dazed, they were back some thirty hours later.

One afternoon, the gates of my shed opened and three men came in.

'It's Maci. It's Maci. It's Maci ...' Whispers were flowing from those at the front of the shed towards those of us closer to its end.

Until this moment, all three men, Maci, his brother Emir, and their neighbour Mirsad, were thought to be dead. Maci and Emir had refused to surrender and they remained in the area. They had witnessed the Chetniks from Radivojci plundering abandoned houses. Several times, they were spotted and fired upon, but each time they had managed to escape.

After more than four months of hiding, they decided to move towards the Croatian border. Walking across the plains, they had spotted a familiar figure in front of them. It was Mirsad, who had been hiding for two months on his own. For two months he had not spoken to another human being. He was on his way to sneak through the enemy lines to Croatia. They got rid of their firearms.

Reaching the border, Maci had made a disastrous mistake. He was thirsty and he insisted on going to a nearby house to get some water. The others tried to talk him out of it, but he refused to listen. He went straight to the only Serb house in an otherwise Muslim village. The Serb informed the Chetniks, and the men were captured by the local police.

There were three escapes from Manjaca — two of them successful. The first one was a man who worked in different areas outside the wire for a long time. This had given him an opportunity to learn a lot about the area around the camp. He was young and strong, and it was a long way to freedom as the whole region had fallen into Serb hands. He was never caught.

The next escape was even more spectacular. The brain that planned it was the ex-convict, Muhamed Sahbaz. For weeks, he had been buying food to improve his physical condition. Very often I saw him in the kitchen, snatching a whole loaf of bread before the very noses of the kitchen staff — although he was never caught. He teamed up with another man, and as part of their grand plan they volunteered to work in the forest. They did not come back in the evening. During the evening count, it was found that they were missing — by which time they were miles away.

Days passed and we did not expect to see them back, but they were eventually caught. While on the run, on their way to Kozarac, they were stopped by a Serb peasant who wondered who they were and what they were doing there.

'We are former prisoners from Manjaca,' they said. 'The camp was closed a couple of days ago, and we are going home.' They managed to get away.

When they reached Prijedor, they even went to the Balkan Hotel — which stood at the busiest spot in town — and had a beer there.

'Where on earth did they manage to get the money?' I wondered. But Muhamed was a resourceful man.

When they eventually reached Kozarac, they slept in the ruins of Muhamed's house. In the morning, they picked some plums in his garden, and then they headed towards the Croatian border. They were caught at the border attempting to cross the Sava River.

Back in Manjaca, Muhamed was repeatedly beaten. His body was badly bruised and his head swollen, and he was no longer able to walk on his own. The Chetniks finally left him alone after repeated protests by the ICRC.

The third escape worked perfectly well. A young sheep farmer from Jajce had been incarcerated for a relatively short time. Being a sheep farmer, he had managed to get the job of looking after the sheep in the closely guarded area around the camp. One day, he and a friend of his were gone. Their absence was not noticed until the following morning.

Their escape had been carefully planned. Several days earlier, they had bought extra blankets and some food. When asked by an inmate: 'Why do you need these?' they replied: 'We're going to run away.'

Everybody laughed, and nobody took it seriously. Just before the gates of their shed were closed, using the cover of the darkness, they nipped out. They threw the blankets on the barbed wire and crossed it — avoiding the mines. They had prepared two horses earlier. The area was well known to the sheep farmer. For many years, he and his father had moved their flocks of sheep all over Bosnia. He was thus able to avoid all the places inhabited by the enemy.

The following morning, the sheep farmer's father was interrogated. He persistently claimed he knew nothing about the escape.

For the rest of us, things did not look good. Everybody was saying, 'We will be released soon. It's not possible to survive up here in winter.'

Others heard rumours that we would not be released, but would be moved to army barracks in Banja Luka. The temperature was falling. More blankets were delivered — but even wrapped in several blankets, I felt the cold creeping under my skin. With cold concrete beneath me and the brisk winds blowing from all directions through every shed opening, and without any sort of heating, the days ahead looked bleak. Even during the day, we had to spend most of the time walking just to keep warm.

One day, the camp authorities announced they wanted to register every inmate whose relatives could secure him a visa for a foreign country. This indicated some kind of change would take place soon. Several of those who wrote to their families received the necessary papers, but they were not released.

Finally, on November 14, about seven hundred men over forty and under eighteen were released and evacuated under the auspices of the ICRC to Karlovac Reception Centre in Croatia. Two weeks before this, Trnopolje camp was closed. Something was happening. Releases spoke more than words. I started hoping I might be free before the New Year.

Captain Boskovic left in this convoy. While the convoy was leaving, Boskovic threw a pack of cigarettes across the wire to some men standing in the kitchen. Inside the pack, there was a message saying the rest of us would be released in two weeks. The ICRC never gave even a hint of when we might be released. So he must have heard it from the Serbs, who felt free to give him this information outside the camp — but he nevertheless managed to relay it to us. However, after two weeks, about three thousand of us were still freezing as the first snow covered Manjaca.

On December 12, rumours swept through the camp that five hundred extremists were to be transferred to another camp. No one knew what kind of criteria the Serbs used when making this classification. Anxiety filled the air.

The following morning, the sky was bright and the sun soon started rising above the mountain. At that moment, I did not know this was the sun I had waited to see for two hundred and two days. It was nearing ten o'clock when a guard came to our shed. He briefly explained that those called out should leave the shed with their possessions, and run to the assembly point in front of the gates. My mate Ekro was called. A couple of days earlier, Himzo, Ekro, and I had agreed that whichever of the three of us left the camp first, he would give a pack of cigarettes to the other two. Neither Himzo nor I thought of the promised cigarettes. It was not a moment for such thoughts. We were saying our last goodbye to Ekro, but he remembered and said: 'Whoever leaves first, leaves a pack behind.'

If I had known where he was going, I would not only have refused to accept the cigarettes, I would have given him my pack, too. In the months to come, he would need them far more than either Himzo or I. For the two of us, freedom was less than thirty hours away.

Amongst the men selected was the new head of the camp, Sarajlic. He must have known about our release, for he desperately tried to stay with us. Somebody finally intervened on his behalf and he was allowed to stay. Ekro and five hundred and thirty-one others were sent to the Batkovic camp near Bijeljina.

'That's it for today,' I said to myself and started thinking about lunch. I did not know that it was just beginning.

A loud command echoed throughout the camp, instructing everyone to leave his shed. We gathered around a guard holding several lists in his hands. Adrenalin shot to my head. 'This is it,' I thought.

The same scene was being played out in Camp One. The procedure required quick responses. When called out, one instantly had to give one's father's name and one's own date of birth. These details were a passport to freedom. All thoughts about food disappeared. I was all ears. Those incarcerated first were at the top of the list. May 26, my day of detention, was the earliest date registered by the ICRC.

Kasim was called before me. I was called fifteen minutes later. I left the camp gates and joined a group at the back. In front of me, there were eleven separate groups — each one numbering sixty men. We had to remember the number of the group, our line, and our position in the line — for we were to board buses the next morning in this same order. On my right side, between us and the bungalows, there was a table with some papers on it. A soldier standing there briefly explained that the following morning we would be released, but could not remain in Bosnia.

'Is there anyone here who does not want to leave tomorrow?' he asked. But everyone remained silent. 'Before your release, you'll have to sign papers leaving all your property to the Serbian Republic, stating that you don't wish to return to your homes.' We were still silent.

The sun set behind the mountain and the lights came on. By five o'clock we were back inside the wire. Lunch was finished. We were given a loaf of bread and two cans of sardines each — one for dinner and one for breakfast.

This was to be one of the longest nights of my life. At around 7.00pm, the shed deputies distributed jumpers and jackets brought in by the ICRC. Everyone received a jumper, but several hundred remained short of a jacket. The missing jackets had been very carefully selected by the guards while we were still standing in the line. I saw them opening the boxes and choosing the ones they liked best. It did not bother me at all. Tomorrow afternoon, I would be free.

When the shed gates closed, an unusually large number of oil lamps remained alight. Everybody was excited. Those of us leaving the next morning could not wait to see the first signs of daylight. Those staying behind, our neighbours, friends, and often brothers, could not sleep either. Even though we talked louder than usual, no warnings came from the guards. I fell asleep around 4.00am. It seemed no more than ten minutes, and I was awake again.

The gates opened and those staying behind started going to the kitchen for their breakfast. I opened my fish can and ate it all. I did not care how long this last journey was going to take. I could put up with hunger for one more day. Kasim and Himzo sitting next to me did the same. Soon after, an order arrived for us to leave the camp. Instead of saying goodbye to those staying behind we said: 'See you soon in Karlovac.'

I passed through the camp gates for the last time. I was split from Kasim and Himzo, who joined their assigned groups. The buses for our transport were late. With time, it became obvious that this was a deliberate procrastination ploy on the part of the Serbs. After several hours of delay, the first buses started arriving. The ICRC wanted the whole group to leave at the same time, so we had to wait for the rest of the buses.

It was already afternoon when finally, all the buses arrived. We started boarding. The ICRC made sure we got on the right bus and a young man with long hair was advising everyone: 'Don't give interviews to reporters in Croatia. It may work against those staying behind you. Good luck.' He shook hands with us.

Each bus was supposed to be protected by an escort, but only a few had one. We had only a Serb driver who did not speak to us throughout the whole journey.

On each seat, the ICRC had placed a small bag with a pack of biscuits, a chocolate, and an apple. Next to them was a pack of cigarettes. Some unlucky ones found their cigarettes missing. It must have been the guards or the bus driver. We collected donations, and each of us gave up a cigarette to make sure that the unlucky ones had their packs, too. When the last person had boarded, the column started moving. Those staying behind waved to us from the Camp One kitchen.

I had a last look at two quiet friends — two wild pear trees standing on opposite sides of the road. So long, my friends. Whenever I entered the kitchen, my eyes had rested on these two trees that I had come to like so much. If there was anything I wanted to take from this place with me, it was those two pear trees. Whenever I travel back to Manjaca in my thoughts, I say hello to these two quiet friends. The memory of them will never fade away.

Groups of reporters standing along the road were filming the convoy. There were also Chetnik irregulars with their long beards laughing at us. Further on, the road became steeper. I turned back to look at the mountain peak which dominated the whole place. The further we moved towards the Vrbas Valley, the more snowy peaks came into view.

Almost the entire area along the road was uninhabited. I spotted only some small groups of houses. Approaching the first group, the convoy stopped and a police vehicle drove ahead. It seemed like a precautionary measure against a possible ambush. Moving again, we saw angry locals but could not hear them. They waved their fists in the air, threatening. Children as small as three wore Chetnik caps, and raised three fingers in the air. Many bitter thoughts rushed through my mind in those couple of minutes. If children of this age were taught to hate members of a different ethnic group, how could there ever be peace?

The convoy stopped again for a short while at Seher, the old part of Banja Luka that had been entirely populated by Muslims. We moved on. There were not many people around. The place swarmed with police and soldiers. A few old men and women cried and secretly waved to us. An old man waved to us openly and a policeman immediately approached him asking him questions. Across the Vrbas River, two mosques lay in ruins. What had happened in Prijedor months before was now well under way in Banja Luka. The town that once used to be the residence of Bosnian viziers was now under the unbridled control of the Chetniks. One of the viziers, Ferhad Pasa, left as a legacy one of the oldest and most beautiful mosques in the whole of Bosnia. It was soon to meet the same fate as hundreds of other mosques.

In Klasnice, the convoy was stopped by about a hundred and fifty Chetniks armed to the teeth. They blocked our route and demanded that we return back to Manjaca. Their leader was Radivoj, a Serb from Trnopolje. A hundred and fifty of them, armed as they were, could massacre us all in a matter of seconds. We stood there for about twenty minutes, when a group of white UN vehicles arrived. The UN soldiers made it quite clear to the Chetniks that they had to let us through, or they would open the road by force.

After this, we expected roadblocks at every turn. The region was full of irregular militia groups and we knew that their behaviour was highly unpredictable. We felt vulnerable, afraid to be in this dangerous area after dark. However, the rest of the journey was uninterrupted. We passed through peaceful areas inhabited by Serbs. There were no traces of fighting there.

Finally, Gradiska.

Crossing the bridge, we left Bosnia having 'willingly agreed' not to return — and leaving all our properties to the Serbian Republic.